THESE THINGS WE BELIEVE

These Things
WE BELIEVE

J. CLYDE TURNER

Convention Press

NASHVILLE　　　　　TENNESSEE

This book is the text for course 05003 in
the subject area Baptist Doctrine
in the Church Study Course

Dewey Decimal Classification Number: 230.6
Library of Congress Card Number: 56–23822
Printed in the United States of America

Church Training Department
Sunday School Board, SBC
127 Ninth Avenue, North
Nashville, Tennessee 37234

ABOUT THE AUTHOR

Dr. J. Clyde Turner has had a long and distinguished career as a preacher of the gospel. Many phases of denominational work have been blessed by his outstanding leadership.

Dr. Turner was born in Iredell County, North Carolina, March 31, 1878. He graduated from Wake Forest College in 1899 with an A.B. degree. After teaching in the city schools of Durham, North Carolina, for three years, he was connected with the Masonic Orphanage, Oxford, North Carolina, for the term 1901–1902. Following this service he entered the Southern Baptist Theological Seminary, Louisville, Kentucky, to prepare for the gospel ministry. He graduated with a Th.M. degree in 1905.

Dr. Turner has been pastor of four churches in his long career, serving at Fisherville, Kentucky, during his seminary days; the First Baptist Church, Newport, Kentucky, 1905–1907; the Tattnall Square Baptist Church, Macon, Georgia, 1907–1910; and the First Baptist Church, Greensboro, North Carolina, 1910–1948.

Many distinguished positions of denominational leadership have been held by Dr. Turner. He was a member of the Board of Trustees of Wake Forest College for a quarter of a century. He served as a member of the Board of Trustees of the Southern Baptist Theological Seminary for twenty-five years. Eight of these years he served as president of the Board.

Dr. Turner is the author of a number of other books; among them are: *New Testament Doctrine of the Church, Soul-Winning Doctrines,* and *The Gospel of the Grace of God.*

v

AUTHOR'S PREFACE

THE SUBJECT of this discussion is not "These Things We Understand" but "These Things We Believe." There are many things we believe, though we do not fully understand them. Understanding comes through mental processes, but we believe some things through experience and revelation.

Not all people believe all things that are set forth in this book. There are differences of opinion among men as to what they believe. And not all Baptists believe all that is written in these pages. Since Baptists have no authoritative creed, no one can speak for all Baptists concerning the things they believe. But there are certain fundamental truths to which Baptists in general subscribe.

The Scripture quotations used are taken from the American Standard Version except when otherwise indicated. The American Standard Version is copyrighted by the International Council of Religious Education and is used by permission.

J. CLYDE TURNER

CONTENTS

vii

1

That Wonderful Book

"Thy testimonies are wonderful" (Psalm 119:129).

"THE BIBLE" is the name given to that body of sacred writings called "The Holy Scriptures." It is sometimes designated as "The Holy Bible," because it has the Holy Spirit as its author, and because it deals with holy things.

The word "Bible" is a transliteration of the Greek *biblos,* which means book. The Bible is *the* Book. There are many books in the world, but the Bible is the only one that has the right to be called "The Book." It is different from all other books.

An educated Chinese to whom a copy of the Scriptures had been given came to the missionary and said: "What is there about this book that you gave me that is different? In all my reading of Chinese literature I have read many good precepts, but never, until I read this book, have I been troubled in my mind when I have done wrong. Now, whenever I do wrong, I am troubled. Why is this book different from all other books that I have read?"

William E. Gladstone, the great English statesman, said, "The Bible is stamped with a specialty of origin, and an immeasurable distance separates it from all competitors."

The Bible is more than a book; it is a library containing sixty-six books. It has been called "the divine library." In it are found books of law, history, biography, poetry, and prophecy.

The psalmist had but a small portion of the Old Testament as his Bible, but to him it was a wonderful book. "Thy testimonies are wonderful." How much more wonderful is the

1

complete Bible which we have! What is there about the Bible
that makes it so wonderful?

I. An Inspired Book

The Bible is the only book in all the world that can claim
to be inspired in the true meaning of the word.

1. *The Meaning of Inspiration*

By inspiration we mean more than spiritual illumination
and exaltation, which come to many. The word "inspire"
comes from a Latin word which means to breathe on, or
breathe in. The Bible is inspired in the sense that it was
written by men who were inbreathed by the Holy Spirit. That
is what Peter meant when he said: "But men spake from God,
being moved by the Holy Spirit" (2 Peter 1:21). The Bible
was written by men, but they were men who were guided by
the Holy Spirit.

Inspiration does not mean that all parts of the Bible are of
equal importance. The book of Leviticus, which gives the
ceremonial law, is not as important as the book of Romans,
which reveals God's great plan of salvation. The tenth chapter of Genesis, which gives a list of names, is not comparable
to the third chapter of John, which presents a Saviour's love.
But every part of the Bible has its own place and makes its
contribution to the whole. God's revelation is progressive in
nature. The Old Testament forms the background for the
New Testament.

Inspiration does not mean that the writers made no effort
to get the facts about which they were writing. Luke, in the
preface of his Gospel, says: "It seemed good to me also, having traced the course of all things accurately from the first, to
write unto thee in order, most excellent Theophilus" (Luke
1:3). He made diligent effort to ascertain the facts, but he
was divinely guided in his efforts.

The Bible was written in the Hebrew and Greek languages —the Old Testament in the Hebrew, and the New Testament in the Greek. In olden days the only way of reproducing the Scriptures was to copy the manuscripts by hand, a long and tedious process. The original manuscripts were lost, and all we have today are copies of copies of the original writings. Our English Bible is a translation of these copies. It was the original Scriptures that were inspired, as holy men of God were borne along by the Holy Spirit. There is every evidence that the integrity of the original Scriptures has been preserved in a wonderful way.

2. *The Method of Inspiration*

Not all Christians agree as to the method of inspiration. Not all Baptists are in agreement on the subject. In the main, there are two schools of thought which we simply record here for information:

(1) *Mechanical inspiration.*—Some believe in plenary, verbal, inspiration, that is, that every word of the Bible was dictated by the Holy Spirit, either directly or indirectly. The men wrote exactly what God told them to write. In Exodus 24:4, we read: "And Moses wrote all the words of Jehovah." Again, in Jeremiah 30:1-2, "The word that came to Jeremiah from Jehovah, saying, Thus speaketh Jehovah, the God of Israel, saying, Write thee all the words that I have spoken unto thee in a book." And Paul said: "But we received, not the spirit of the world, but the spirit which is from God; that we might know the things that were freely given to us of God. Which things also we speak, not in words which man's wisdom teacheth, but which the Spirit teacheth" (1 Cor. 2:12-13).

It is also true that the writers did not always understand the full significance of the things they wrote. Isaiah and the other prophets did not fully comprehend all that they wrote about the events of the future. They were writing what God told them to write. "Concerning which salvation the prophets sought and searched diligently, who prophesied of the grace that should come unto you: searching what time or what manner of time the Spirit of Christ which was in them did point unto, when it testified beforehand the sufferings of Christ, and the glories that should follow them" (1 Peter 1:10–11).

(2) *Dynamical inspiration.*—This may be called thought inspiration, as opposed to verbal inspiration. According to this theory, the words were chosen by the writers, but the truth expressed was from God. This gives opportunity for the writers to express their own individuality, and explains the differences in style found in the different writings.

Whatever may have been the method of inspiration, the men who wrote the Bible were divinely guided so that they wrote what God wanted them to say. Dr. A. H. Strong expresses it this way: "The Scripture writers appear to have been so influenced by the Holy Spirit that they perceived and felt even the new truths they were to publish, as discoveries of their own minds, and were left to the action of their own minds in the expression of these truths, with the single exception that they were supernaturally held back from the selection of wrong words, and when needful were provided with right ones. Inspiration is therefore verbal as to its result, but not verbal as to its method." [1]

3. *The Evidences of Inspiration*

What evidence do we have that the Bible is an inspired book?

(1) *The Bible claims.*—The men who wrote the Bible claimed that they were speaking for God, or that God was speaking through them. "Hear, O heavens, and give ear, O earth; for Jehovah hath spoken" (Isa. 1:2). "Now the word

[1] *Systematic Theology,* p. 103

of Jehovah came unto me, saying, . . ." (Jer. 1:4). "For I make known to you, brethren, as touching the gospel which was preached by me, that it is not after man. For neither did I receive it from man, nor was I taught it, but it came to me through revelation of Jesus Christ" (Gal. 1:11–12). Paul declared: "Every scripture inspired of God is also profitable" (2 Tim. 3:16). The Authorized Version reads: "All scripture is given by inspiration of God," and Dr. A. T. Robertson says this is the more natural meaning. There are many other passages which claim inspiration for the Scriptures.

(2) *The unity of the Bible.*—The Bible was not written by one man, but by many men, representing different walks of life—shepherds, farmers, fishermen, kings, and peasants. It was not all written in the same age. There is a period of about sixteen hundred years between the writing of the first and last books of the Bible. Neither was it all written in one place. Parts of it were written in the wilderness, parts in Palestine, and other parts in various places, from Rome to Babylon. The original manuscripts were not written with the purpose of forming one book. Each writer worked independently. And yet, when these writings were collected under the guidance of the Holy Spirit, they formed one book of remarkable unity. There is but one explanation, the guiding hand of God was in it.

(3) *The contents of the Bible.*—The Bible contains truths, prophecies, and a message to man which could not have been the mere product of human minds.

First, there are truths set forth in the Bible which men could never have known if they had not been divinely revealed. Nature reveals some things about God, but the full truth concerning his nature and purposes could be known only through the inspired record he has given in his Word. And there are truths which cannot be understood unless they are spiritually discerned: "Now the natural man receiveth not the things of the Spirit of God: for they are foolishness unto him; and he cannot know them, because they are spiritually judged" (1 Cor. 2:14).

Second, the fulfilment of prophecy bears witness to the inspiration of the Scriptures. The Old Testament contains prophecies which were not fulfilled until many centuries later. The place and manner of the birth of Jesus were foretold seven hundred years before it came to pass. The fifty-third chapter of Isaiah contains a wonderful description of the sufferings and death of the Lord. We find this expression many times concerning events recorded in the Gospels: "That it might be fulfilled which was spoken of the Lord by the prophet." In the synagogue at Nazareth, Jesus read from the sixty-first chapter of Isaiah; then he closed the book and said: "To-day hath this scripture been fulfilled in your ears" (Luke 4:21). How could men look into the future and tell with certainty and accuracy things that were to come to pass? There is but one answer: they were divinely inspired.

Third, the message of the Bible attests its inspiration. It was said of Jesus: "Never man so spake" (John 7:46). That was true because there was never man like that man. In like manner, it may be said of the Bible: "Never book spake like this Book," because there has never been a book like this Book. It tells us the kind of God we have; it reveals the awful nature and consequences of sin; it points out the way of salvation. Its teachings have been the source of the world's highest spiritual ideals and moral standards. Without the Bible, men would be left groping in spiritual darkness.

(4) *The testimony of Jesus.*—The words of Jesus confirm the inspiration of the Bible. He often quoted the Scriptures of the Old Testament as having divine authority. "Jesus saith unto them, Did ye never read in the scriptures, The stone which the builders rejected, the same was made the head of the corner; this was from the Lord, and it is marvellous in our eyes?" (Matt. 21:42). "Jesus answered and said unto them, Ye do err, not knowing the scriptures, nor the power of

God" (Matt. 22:29). "And beginning from Moses and from
all the prophets, he interpreted to them in all the scriptures
the things concerning himself" (Luke 24: 27).

Men have questioned the inspiration of the Old Testament
Scriptures, but there seems to have been no question in the
mind of Jesus. He took two events out of the Old Testament
concerning which doubts have been raised, and used them
to illustrate eternal truths. Concerning the flood, he said:
"For as in those days which were before the flood they were
eating and drinking, marrying and giving in marriage, until
the day that Noah entered into the ark, and they knew not
until the flood came, and took them all away; so shall be the
coming of the Son of man" (Matt. 24:38–39).

Some have made light of the story of Jonah and the whale,
but Jesus said: "For as Jonah was three days and three nights
in the belly of the whale; so shall the Son of man be three
days and three nights in the heart of the earth" (Matt.
12:40). In his last discourse to his disciples before his death,
Jesus said: "In my Father's house are many mansions; if it
were not so, I would have told you" (John 14:2). He would
not allow them to entertain hopes if those hopes were not to
be fulfilled. The words may be given a wider application. If
the Scriptures which they believed had not been true, he
would have told them.

The promise which Jesus gave to his disciples assured the
inspiration of the New Testament Scriptures: "But the Comforter, even the Holy Spirit, whom the Father will send in
my name, he shall teach you all things, and bring to your re-
membrance all that I said unto you" (John 14:26). That explains how the writers could quote the long discourses of
Jesus many years after they were uttered.

Again Jesus said: "I have yet many things to say unto you,
but ye cannot bear them now. Howbeit when he, the Spirit
of truth, is come, he shall guide you into all the truth: for he
shall not speak from himself; but what things soever he shall

hear, these shall he speak: and he shall declare unto you the
things that are to come" (John 16:12–13).

(5) *The influence of the Bible.*—Wherever the Bible has
gone, it has brought about changes in the lives of men and of
nations. Under its influence, sinners have been transformed
into saints, and nations have been changed from savages into
sons of God. It has brought comfort to sorrowing hearts, and
courage to souls in despair.

All that is best in literature, music, and art can be traced
to the influence of the Bible. George Washington said: "It is
impossible to rightly govern the world without God and the
Bible."

John R. Green says: "No greater moral change ever passed
over a nation than passed over England during the years
which parted the middle of the reign of Elizabeth from the
meeting of the Long Parliament. England became the people
of a book, and that book was the Bible." [2]

II. A Religious Book

The Bible does not deal with all realms of truth. It was
not designed to teach science and other branches of learning.
It is primarily a religious book, pointing men to God and
teaching them how to live. As a religious book, several truths
concerning the Bible are to be emphasized.

1. *Authoritative*

The Bible is authoritative in the realm of religion. Some
have placed the seat of authority in the church. They claim
that it is the church which sets forth what men are to believe,
and how they must live. According to this view, the seat of
authority is really in those who are high officials in the
church.

[2] *Short History of the English People,* p. 460

Others attribute partial authority to the Bible. They say it contains the seed of truth, but it must be supplemented by the decrees of men. To those holding this view, the Bible is authoritative in the essential things, but not in the nonessentials. But who will draw the line between the essentials and the nonessentials? The Bible itself has drawn no such line. It is authoritative in all things concerning which it speaks.

There are others who reject the authority of the Bible, and look to the individual conscience and human reason for religious authority. In their view only that is to be accepted as true which appeals to reason, and is approved by conscience. Such a view leaves men with no authority beyond themselves. Every man is his own authority.

Paul, in describing his manner of life before his conversion, said: "I verily thought with myself that I ought to do many things contrary to the name of Jesus of Nazareth. And this I also did in Jerusalem: and I both shut up many of the saints in prisons, having received authority from the chief priests, and when they were put to death I gave my vote against them" (Acts 26:9-10). He was following both the authority of religious leaders and the authority of his own conscience. He was doing what the religious officials told him to do, and what he felt in his heart he ought to do.

If the Bible is divinely inspired, then it is authoritative in its message. When it speaks, it is to be obeyed. More than once, as he combatted the errors of religious leaders, Paul appealed to the Scriptures. As he spoke in the synagogue at Thessalonica, he "reasoned with them from the scriptures" (Acts 17:2). In his epistle to the Romans, as he sets forth the great doctrines of salvation, we find such expressions as these: "What saith the scriptures?" (4:3), "For the scripture saith" (10:11). It is to the Scriptures we must still go for our authority. When it is a choice between man's word and God's word, "we must obey God rather than men" (Acts 5:29).

2. Sufficient

The Bible is a sufficient guide in all things religious. It does not reveal all religious truth, but it reveals all that is necessary for man to know in order to work out his destiny. It is an all-sufficient rule of faith and practice. It makes known all that is necessary for man to believe, and all that he needs to do. It makes the way of salvation so plain that "the wayfaring men, yea fools, shall not err therein." It reveals God's plan for his church and all of its activities. It points out the manner of life that men and women are to follow. It pulls aside the veil and lets men catch a vision of the world to come.

The Bible is not a book of rules, but of principles. It does not give a "thou shalt," or a "thou shalt not," for every experience of life. Rather, it lays down the great fundamental principles by which men are to be guided in making their own decisions and in shaping their own lives.

3. Final

There will never be another Bible, because there will never be need for another. It contains all that is necessary for man to know down to the end of time. That does not mean that there may not be new interpretations of the Bible and new truths drawn from the Bible. It is inexhaustible in its treasures. No single age has discovered all the truth to be found in it. But it is final in its message.

The world will never outgrow the Bible. In one of his last discourses Jesus said, "Heaven and earth shall pass away, but my words shall not pass away" (Matt. 24:35). Peter declared: "The word of the Lord abideth for ever" (1 Peter 1:25). Jesus said his word would enter into the judgment of the last day: "He that rejecteth me, and receiveth not my sayings, hath one that judgeth him: the word that I spake, the same shall judge him in the last day" (John 12:48).

III. A LIVING AND ACTIVE BOOK

That is the claim which the Bible makes for itself: "For the word of God is living, and active" (Heb. 4:12). It is living and active because it is the word of a living and active God. Peter describes it as "the word of God, which liveth and abideth" (1 Peter 1:23).

Many who were listening over the radio to the coronation service of England's new queen, Elizabeth, heard the archbishop say, as he handed her the Bible: "We present you with this Book, the most valuable thing that this world affords." Following this, the Moderator of the General Assembly of the Church of Scotland said, "Here is Wisdom; This is the royal Law; These are the lively Oracles of God."

Men have tried to kill the Bible, but it still lives. No other book has had so many enemies, who have done all within their power to destroy it. It has been ridiculed by atheists and spurned by unbelievers. Voltaire, the French infidel, prophesied that in a hundred years the Bible would be a forgotten book. Ingersoll went still further. He declared that in ten years the Bible would not be read, and in twenty years it would be a forgotten book. But the bodies of these men have long lain in the dust, and their names well-nigh forgotten, while the Bible still lives and continues to be the world's best seller.

That the Bible is a living and active book, is shown by the figures that are used to describe it.

1. *Seed*

This is the figure which Jesus used: "The seed is the word of God" (Luke 8:11). A seed is something that has life. Some years ago the story was spread abroad that some seed, which had laid for centuries in an Egyptian tomb, were found to have life in them still, and, when planted, they sprouted and brought forth grain. I know not how true that story is, but I do know that the seed which is the Word of God, though many centuries old, is a living thing, and, when planted in a human heart, brings forth fruit.

I read of an old professor of botany who used to hold a little brown seed in his hand and say to his class: "I know the exact composition in this seed. It has in it hydrogen, carbon, and nitrogen. I know the exact proportions, and can make a seed that looks exactly like it. If I plant my seed, it will come to naught; its elements will soon be absorbed in the soil. But if I plant the seed which God has made, it will become a plant, because it contains the mysterious principle we call the life principle."

In like manner, men may make a book that looks like the Bible. It may be printed on the same kind of paper and bound in the same kind of material. But there is a vast difference. The Word of God has life in it, and, when planted in good soil, it will produce a harvest.

A seed not only has life in it, it has power; it is active. As it springs up from the soil, it pushes every obstacle out of the way. It is a common sight to see a large stone, too heavy for a man to lift, pushed aside, and sometimes rent asunder, by a growing plant springing from a tiny seed which has lodged in a crevice in the rock.

2. *Light*

The psalmist said: "Thy word is a lamp unto my feet, and light unto my path" (Psalm 119:105). The Word of God is both a lamp and a light. Men are pilgrims, traveling along an unknown way. They need a light to reveal the way ahead, and they need a lamp, or lantern, to reveal the nature of the ground over which they are walking, to point out the stumbling stones and pitfalls. In the Word of God they find that light and that lamp. Those who walk in its light do not go astray, neither do they stumble and fall. Robert E. Lee once said: "The Bible is a book in comparison with which all others in my eyes are of minor importance, and which in all my perplexities and distresses has never failed to give me light and strength."

3. *Fire*

"Is not my word like fire? saith Jehovah" (Jer. 23:29). Fire is an agent of both cleansing and destruction. Metals are put into the fire in order that the dross and impurities may be burned away, and the metals purified. The Word of God is both a destructive and purifying agent. To those who reject it, it becomes "a savor from death unto death," but to those who obey it, it becomes "a savor from life unto life."

The prophet was probably emphasizing the purifying power of the Word. The psalmist recognized the power of God's Word to cleanse, when he said: "Wherewith shall a young man cleanse his way? By taking heed thereto according to thy word" (Psalm 119:9).

4. *Hammer*

The prophet realized that God's Word was not only like a fire, but also "like a hammer that breaketh the rock in pieces" (Jer. 23:29).

We call the fifth day of the week "Thursday," which means Thor's day. Thor was one of the Scandinavian gods. He had three wonderful things with which he worked: a belt which doubled his strength, a pair of gloves, and a hammer so heavy that no mortal could lift it. With that mighty hammer he struck down giants and gained victories.

That is legend, but it is no legend that the Word of God is a mighty hammer which breaks rocks to pieces. The unbeliever's heart is described in the Word of God as being a heart of stone. The Word of God is the hammer with which such stony hearts are broken. Under the power of the Word, hearts of stone become "broken and contrite hearts."

A man went to hear D. L. Moody preach, with the intention of finding things to criticize. But he came away a changed man. In telling about it, he said: "Mr. Moody just stood there and pounded me with verse after verse of Scripture until it got under my skin."

5. *Sword*

"And the sword of the Spirit, which is the word of God" (Eph. 6:17). This may mean, either the sword which the Spirit uses, or the sword which the Spirit furnishes. Both are true. The Word of God is the sword which the Spirit uses to bring conviction, regeneration, and sanctification. With that Word, he comforts sorrowing hearts and brings courage to despairing souls.

But the Word of God is also the sword which the Spirit provides for the Christian warrior. It is his weapon of defense and offense. It is with the Word that men are to ward off temptation.

Our Lord gave us the example. When the devil assailed him with his strongest temptation, Jesus did not argue with him but said: "It is written," and proceeded to quote from the Word of God. After three attempts the devil withdrew in defeat.

The psalmist found the best method of withstanding temptation: "Thy word have I laid up in my heart, that I might not sin against thee" (Psalm 119:11).

The Word of God is also the Christian's weapon of offense. With that sword he is to go forth and win victories. In 1870 a native missionary of the Hawaiian Islands stood before a great throng of people, among whom were members of the royal family and other dignitaries. He lifted a copy of God's Word in his hand and said: "Not with powder and ball, not with sword and cannon, but with the living Word of God and his Spirit do we go forth to conquer these islands for Christ." It is with that mighty sword the church is to win this world to Christ. The words of exhortation which Paul gave to a young preacher in the long ago ring down the centuries and say to the preachers of this day: "Preach the word."

Truly, the Bible is a wonderful book.

> And better had they ne'er been born,
> Who read to doubt, or read to scorn.
>
> SCOTT

2

The One True God

"For I am God, and there is none else" (Isa. 45:22).

BELIEF in the existence of a divine being is well-nigh universal. There are very few people who profess to believe that there is no God. The Bible characterizes such people as fools: "The fool hath said in his heart, There is no God" (Psalm 53:1). Dr. E. Y. Mullins used to say, "He said it in his heart; his head knew better." Everything around us, and above us, bears witness to the existence of God. "The heavens declare the glory of God; and the firmament showeth his handiwork" (Psalm 19:1).

It is said of Napoleon that one night he sat listening to an argument among his officers. Some of them were ridiculing religion. Others went further, denying the existence of God. Presently Napoleon arose and stood in their midst. Pointing to the stars above, he said: "Gentlemen, you may conceivedly be right; but, if so, who made those stars?"

While most people acknowledge the existence of God, they differ widely in their conception of him. Some have fashioned a god out of their own imagination, and according to their own desires. Some look upon him as a kind of superman, having the form and nature of man. Others look upon him as an impersonal force that pervades the universe. There is but one place to which we can go to find a true conception of God, and that is the Bible, in which he reveals himself.

The Bible makes no effort to prove the existence of God. It opens with the declaration, "In the beginning God created the heavens and the earth." In the beginning of what? It

17

is evident that the words refer to the beginning of what we call "time," the beginning of the material universe.

What does the Bible reveal about God?

I. God's Name

When we use the word "God," there is no question as to the meaning. We are thinking of the one Supreme Being, Creator and Sovereign of all things. But, in the conception of the people of old, there were many gods. Paul says: "For though there be that are called gods, whether in heaven or on earth; as there are gods many, and lords many" (1 Cor. 8:5). Every nation had its own god. Some of them worshiped many gods, called by different names.

God gave himself a name by which he was to be known, as distinct from other gods: "I am Jehovah, that is my name" (Isa. 42:8). He first revealed that name to Moses when he commissioned him to lead the children of Israel from Egyptian bondage: "Thus shalt thou say unto the children of Israel, Jehovah, the God of your fathers, the God of Abraham, the God of Isaac, and the God of Jacob, hath sent me unto you: this is my name for ever, and this is my memorial unto all generations" (Ex. 3:15). In Exodus 6:2–3 he says he had not been known by that name before: "And God spake unto Moses, and said unto him, I am Jehovah: and I appeared unto Abraham, unto Isaac, and unto Jacob, as God Almighty; but by my name Jehovah I was not known to them." They had known something of that name, for Abraham called the place where he went to offer up Isaac as a burnt offering, "Jehovah-jireh" (Gen. 22:14). But they had not known the full significance of the name. It took on new meaning as it was revealed to Moses. It was God's covenant name, his redemptive name.

Several things are to be noted about this name which God gave to himself.

1. *A Personal Name*

There were many so-called gods in the days of Israel. Each nation had its own god. And these gods had personal names. The god of the Moabites was Chemosh (Kemosh). The god of the Ammonites was Molech (Molek). The god of the Zidonians was Baal. But the name of the God of the Hebrews was Jehovah: "I am Jehovah, that is my name."

2. *A Descriptive Name*

In those early days, names that were descriptive of character were given to people. Jacob was the name given to the second-born son of Isaac and Rebekah, because that represented his character—a supplanter. This name was changed to Israel when he became a prince of God. So the name Jehovah was descriptive of God's character. It carries with it the idea of eternity of being and unchangeableness of character. When Moses asked God what name he should give to him when he told the children of Israel, "The God of your fathers hath sent me unto you," God said: "Thus shalt thou say unto the children of Israel, I AM hath sent me unto you" (Ex. 3:14). This comes from the same root as Jehovah. Jehovah is the great "I AM." With him there is no past, and no present, and no future. All is one eternal now. He is the eternal God, the unchangeable God, the same yesterday, today, and forever. "From everlasting to everlasting, thou art God" (Psalm 90:2).

3. *A Sacred Name*

When God gave the Ten Commandments to Israel, he said: "I am Jehovah thy God" (Ex. 20:2). Then, in the Third Commandment, he said: "Thou shalt not take the name of Jehovah thy God in vain; for Jehovah will not hold him guiltless that taketh his name in vain" (Ex. 20:7). In giving the Model Prayer, Jesus said: "Our Father who art in heaven,

Hallowed be thy name" (Matt. 6:9). Because it was such a sacred name, the Jews refused to take it on their lips. They substituted "Lord" for it.

4. *A Memorial Name*

God said to Moses, upon revealing to him his name: "This is my name for ever, and this is my memorial [name] unto all generations." It was a memorial of his gracious dealings with the children of Israel in bringing them out of bondage. In all future generations, when his name should be mentioned, it would be a reminder of his redemptive work in Egypt, which was a foretoken of his redemptive work at Calvary.

II. GOD'S NATURE

What kind of being is God?

1. *Some Descriptive Words*

We find in the Bible four definite statements which are descriptive of God.

(1) *Spirit.*—This is the statement which Jesus made: "God is a Spirit" (John 4:24). God is not a superman, with a body of flesh; he is a Spirit being. He is free from all the limitations which a body imposes.

The biblical passages which ascribe to God bodily parts, such as arms, eyes, and hands, have led many to look upon him as having a body something like our bodies. Some people would picture him as a grand old man, sitting on his throne in the heavens. It is hard for finite minds to think of God without ascribing to him some bodily form. But such a being would be limited in many ways. God is Spirit, hence free from all limitations.

As Spirit, God is a living God. He is so described in the Bible: "Jehovah is the true God; he is the living God" (Jer.

10:10); "And how ye turned unto God from idols, to serve a living and true God" (1 Thess. 1:9). As the living God, he not only has life in himself, he is the source of life.

As Spirit, God is a personal God, a self-conscious, self-determining, and moral being. We often associate personality with a body. A person is someone we can see. But personality belongs, not to the body, but to the spirit. It is because God is a personal being that we can have fellowship with him.

(2) *Light.*—This is the description which John gave of God: "God is light, and in him is no darkness at all" (1 John 1:5). Darkness is symbolic of ignorance, and error, and sin. Light symbolizes wisdom and purity. God is an all-wise and perfect being.

(3) *Love.*—Another of the descriptive words which John used is "love." (1 John 4:8). The great and holy God is also a God of love. This is the attribute of God which brings hope to the sinful heart. To know God only as all-powerful and holy would leave the individual in fear and awe. But to know that this great and holy God is a God of love kindles hope in the heart.

God's love is manifest in many ways, but the supreme manifestation is the gift of his Son. "Herein was the love of God manifested in us, that God hath sent his only begotten Son into the world that we might live through him" (1 John 4:9). There are many experiences which might cause men to doubt the love of God, but no one can stand before the cross of Calvary and have any doubts. "God commendeth his own love toward us, in that, while we were yet sinners, Christ died for us" (Rom. 5:8).

(4) *A consuming fire.*— The author of Hebrews (12:29) quotes from Deuteronomy 4:24: "Our God is a consuming fire." God is not only a God of love, but a God of righteousness as well. Some people magnify the love of God but overlook his righteousness. The psalmist pictured him as a God

of infinite love: "Jehovah is merciful and gracious, slow to anger, and abundant in lovingkindness" (Psalm 103 : 8). But in the next verse he said: "He will not always chide; neither will he keep his anger for ever." Men cannot trifle with God, and then escape his righteous judgments.

2. *God Is Infinite*

Perhaps the one word which best describes God is "infinite." The literal meaning is, without end or limitation.

(1) *Eternal.*—God is without beginning or end. He is the eternal God. "From everlasting to everlasting, thou art God" (Psalm 90 : 2). Because the idea of a being without beginning is beyond human understanding, some have stumbled at it. "Where did God come from?" is a question often asked. We speak of an eternal future, a future without end. Our hope is that we shall live forever. It is no harder to believe in a past that had no beginning than it is to believe in a future that will have no end. It is no more difficult to understand how God has lived throughout an eternal past than it is to understand how we shall live throughout an eternal future. God is not limited by time—"A thousand years in thy sight are but as yesterday when it is past" (Psalm 90:4); "One day is with the Lord as a thousand years, and a thousand years as one day" (2 Peter 3:8).

(2) *Omnipresent.*—God is an omnipresent God. That does not mean that he is spread throughout the universe, but the whole of God is present in every place. There are passages of Scripture which seem to localize God: "Our Father who art in heaven" (Matt. 6:9); "O thou that sittest in the heavens" (Psalm 123:1); "Jehovah hath established his throne in the heavens" (Psalm 103:19). These passages, however, are to be taken in a symbolic way, just like those which speak of his hands and arms. God cannot be confined by space or in space.

There are many Scripture verses which declare the omni-presence of God—"Whither shall I go from thy Spirit? Or whither shall I flee from thy presence? If I ascend up into heaven, thou art there: if I make my bed in Sheol, behold, thou art there. If I take the wings of the morning, and dwell in the uttermost parts of the sea; even there shall thy hand lead me, and thy right hand shall hold me" (Psalm 139:7–10); "He is not far from each one of us: for in him we live, and move, and have our being" (Acts 17:27–28).

(3) *Omniscient.*—God is an omniscient God. He knows all things. He knows all the past, all the present, and all the future. And he knows all about everything and every crea-ture. There is nothing hidden from him. The psalmist said: "Thou knowest my downsitting and mine uprising; thou understandest my thought afar off. Thou searchest out my path and my lying down, and art acquainted with all my ways. For there is not a word in my tongue, but, lo, O Je-hovah, thou knowest it altogether" (Psalm 139:2–4).

(4) *Omnipotent.*—God is an omnipotent God. All power belongs to him: "God hath spoken once, twice have I heard this, that power belongeth unto God" (Psalm 62:11). More than once the Scriptures declare that nothing is impossible with God. That is the claim which God makes for himself: "Behold, I am Jehovah, the God of all flesh: is there anything too hard for me?" (Jer. 32:27). Jesus said: "With men this is impossible; but with God all things are possible" (Matt. 19:26).

Of course, this does not mean that God can do things that are contrary to his nature. Paul declared that God could not lie: "In hope of eternal life, which God, who cannot lie, promised before times eternal" (Titus 1:2). Neither does it mean that God can do things that are self-contradictory. That would be a denial of his own nature. Dr. E. Y. Mullins states the truth in this manner: "By the omnipotence of God we mean his unlimited power to do any and all things consistent with his nature and purpose." [1]

3. God Is a Father

There are references to God as Father in Old Testament history: "A father of the fatherless, and a judge of the widows, is God in his holy habitation" (Psalm 68:5); "I will cause them to walk by rivers of waters, in a straight way wherein they shall not stumble; for I am a father to Israel" (Jer. 31:9); "If then I am a father, where is mine honor?" (Mal. 1:6). But it was Jesus who unfolded the truth of the fatherhood of God in all of its fulness and beauty.

In what sense is God a Father? Misunderstanding and misinterpretation here have led to many errors.

(1) *A creative relationship.*—There is a sense in which God is Father of all: Paul said: "We are also his offspring. Being then the offspring of God, we ought not to think that the Godhead is like unto gold, or silver, or stone, graven by art and device of man" (Acts 17:28-29). God is the Father of all only in the sense that he is Creator and Preserver of all. Some have drawn from this truth the doctrine of universal salvation, which is contrary to the Word of God.

(2) *A redemptive relationship.*—In a special sense God is Father of those who have come into spiritual relationship with him through Jesus Christ: "As many as received him, to them gave he the right to become children of God, even to them that believe on his name" (John 1:12).

The Bible mentions three ways by which one becomes a spiritual child of God. Rather, they are three sides of the same experience.

First, we become sons by faith. "Ye are all sons of God, through faith, in Christ Jesus" (Gal. 3:26). No one is a true child of God until he has put his trust in Jesus Christ.

---

[1] *The Christian Religion in its Doctrinal Expression, p. 228*

Second, we are God's children by a spiritual birth. "Who were born, not of blood, nor of the will of the flesh, nor of the will of man, but of God" (John 1:13). One becomes a child of God only through the experience of regeneration, or the new birth.

Third, we are sons of God by adoption. "Ye received not the spirit of bondage again unto fear; but ye received the spirit of adoption, whereby we cry, Abba, Father" (Rom. 8:15).

The fatherhood of God is, for Christians, one of the most comforting doctrines in the Bible. It means that the great, all-wise, all-powerful God is our own Father. As his children, we have his constant love and care: "And [I] will be to you a Father, and ye shall be to me sons and daughters, saith the Lord Almighty" (2 Cor. 6:18). As children of God, we are "heirs of God, and joint-heirs with Christ" (Rom. 8:17).

III. God's Triune Person

God is revealed in the Bible as a triune God, a Trinity. The word "trinity" is not found in the Scriptures. It was first used in the second century by Tertullian to set forth the truth of one God in three persons. The Trinity is one of the greatest of all mysteries. We would never have known it, if it had not been revealed in the Scriptures. The doctrine is suggested in the Old Testament, and clearly revealed in the New Testament. There are two truths implied in the Trinity.

1. *One God*

This truth is stated many times in the Bible: "Hear, O Israel: Jehovah our God is one Jehovah" (Deut. 6:4); "Thus saith Jehovah, the King of Israel, and his Redeemer, Jehovah of hosts: I am the first, and I am the last; and besides me there is no God" (Isa. 44:6); "We know that no idol is anything in the world, and that there is no God but one" (1 Cor.

8:4). So the doctrine of the Trinity does not mean that we have three gods.

2. *In Three Persons*

The one God exists and manifests himself in a threefold way—Father, Son, and Holy Spirit. For want of a better term, we speak of the three persons in the Godhead. These three are one in essence, but distinct in personality.

One person in the Godhead does not act independently of the others. And yet there is a sense in which there have been three manifestations in God's dealings with mankind.

(1) *The Father.*—We have the partial story of his manifestation in the Old Testament. There were special manifestations of the Holy Spirit, and, perhaps, of the Son, in the person of "the angel of the Lord," but it was Jehovah God who was dealing directly with men. This manifestation was marked by three aspects.

First, God was invisible. Men could not see him. From time to time he sent angels to speak with men, but never was it permitted to any man to see God himself. Moses begged for that privilege, but all that was granted to him was to stand in a cleft of the rock and see the glory of God pass by (Ex. 33:18–23). In John 1:18, it is recorded: "No man hath seen God at any time."

Second, God did not come close to men. He dealt with them at a distance. He came down on the mountaintop, and there, veiled in clouds and smoke, he talked with Moses. Concerning the people as a whole, he said: "Take heed to yourselves, that ye go not up into the mount, or touch the border of it: whosoever toucheth the mount shall be surely put to death" (Ex. 19:12). When the tabernacle was built, God promised that his presence would abide in the holy of holies, but none save the high priest could enter it, and that privilege was granted to him but once a year.

Third, the holiness of God was the divine attribute

stressed. The psalmist said, "Let them praise thy great and terrible name: holy is he" (Psalm 99:3). And again: "Exalt ye Jehovah our God, and worship at his footstool: holy is he" (Psalm 99:5). When Isaiah had his vision of the Lord in the Temple, he heard the seraphim singing: "Holy, holy, holy, is Jehovah of hosts" (Isa. 6:3).

(2) *The Son.*—We have this record in the Four Gospels. In this revelation it was God the Son who was dealing directly with men. This period is also marked by three aspects.

First, in the coming of Christ, men found a visible God, one whom they could see. Jesus said to his disciples: "He that hath seen me hath seen the Father" (John 14:9). Again, in John 1:18, we have these words: "No man hath seen God at any time; the only begotten Son, who is in the bosom of the Father, he hath declared him." So, in Jesus Christ, the invisible God became visible.

Second, God came near to men. In the person of his Son, God stepped down from the clouds and came into close relations with men: "The Word became flesh, and dwelt among us (and we beheld his glory, glory as of the only begotten from the Father), full of grace and truth" (John 1:14). In Jesus Christ, God came and lived with men and talked with them face to face.

Third, the love of God was magnified. The key word of this period is John 3:16: "God so loved the world, that he gave his only begotten Son." The God with a "great and terrible name," of whom the psalmist wrote, became a loving Father to his trusting children.

(3) *The Holy Spirit.*—This manifestation began with the events recorded in the second chapter of Acts, and has continued until the present time. When Jesus was talking to his disciples about his departure from the earth, he said: "I will pray the Father, and he shall give you another Comforter, that he may be with you for ever, even the Spirit of truth" (John 14:16–17).

In the person of the Holy Spirit, God comes into even closer relations with his children. He not only abides with them, but dwells in them: "For he abideth with you, and shall be in you" (John 14:17).

In the Holy Spirit the power of God becomes prominent. The risen Lord said to his disciples, "Ye shall receive power, when the Holy Spirit is come upon you" (Acts 1:8).

IV. God's Work

The work of God may be set forth under three heads.

1. *Creation*

The Bible opens with the declaration: "In the beginning God created the heavens and the earth." Then follows an account of the creation, showing the different stages. Creation was of two kinds: things without life, and things with life. Living things were of two kinds: flora and fauna—plant life and animal life. Animal life was of two kinds: lower and higher—beast and man.

Two questions concerning the creation arise.

(1) *The method of creation.*—How did God make the world and all things in it? Various theories have been advanced, but we are driven back to the simple statement: God created it. The word "create" carries with it the idea of bringing something into existence that did not exist before. It is used of God alone in the Scriptures. It is never said of man that he created anything.

It is significant that the word "create" occurs three times in the creation story: (1) In regard to material things—"In the beginning God created the heavens and the earth" (Gen. 1:1). There is no other explanation of the origin of matter. (2) In regard to animal life—"And God created the great sea-monsters, and every living creature that moveth, wherewith the waters swarmed, after their kind, and every winged bird after its kind" (Gen. 1:21). There is no other explanation of the origin of animal life. (3) In regard to man—"And God created man in his own image" (Gen. 1:27). There is no other explanation of the origin of man. God created the material universe, God created animal life, and God created man.

But how did God create these things? The Bible simply states the fact, without revealing the method, other than to say: "God said, . . . and it was so."

"God said, Let there be light: and there was light" (Gen. 1:3).

"God said, Let there be a firmament in the midst of the waters, and let it divide the waters from the waters. And God made the firmament, and divided the waters which were under the firmament from the waters which were above the firmament: and it was so" (Gen. 1:6–7).

"And God said, Let the waters under the heavens be gathered together unto one place, and let the dry land appear: and it was so" (Gen. 1:9).

"And God said, Let the earth put forth grass, herbs yielding seed, and fruit-trees bearing fruit after their kind, wherein is the seed thereof, upon the earth: and it was so" (Gen. 1:11). This is the statement that runs all through the creation story: "God said, . . . and it was so."

This is the explanation of the creation given by the psalmist: "By the word of Jehovah were the heavens made, and all the host of them by the breath of his mouth" (Psalm 33:6); "For he spake, and it was done; he commanded, and it stood fast" (Psalm 33:9).

The author of Hebrews agrees with the psalmist in this explanation of the universe: "By faith we understand that the worlds have been framed by the word of God, so that what is seen hath not been made out of things which appear" (Heb. 11:3).

(2) *The time of creation.*—How long did it take God to

create all things? The Scriptures declare that it was accomplished in six days: "For in six days Jehovah made heaven and earth, the sea, and all that in them is" (Ex. 20 : 11). Were these days the length of our days of twenty-four hours, or did they refer to indefinite periods of time?

The expression "evening and morning" has been interpreted to mean that the days were the same length as the days of the week. However, the other interpretation is probably more in accord with all the facts. The word "day" is used many times in the Scriptures to denote an indefinite period of time, as in "the day of the Lord," "the day of salvation," "the day of wrath," etc. In Genesis 2 : 4 "day" is used to include the whole creation: "In the day that Jehovah God made earth and heaven."

The how and the when of creation are not as important as the fact that God did it in his own way and in his own time. And it is well to remember that the dates appearing in the margin of the King James Version are in no sense a part of the inspired record. They were arranged by Archbishop Usher of England, in the seventeenth century.

2. *Preservation*

God not only made all things, but he upholds all things and controls all things. He did not create the universe and then withdraw from it. He established certain laws by which the universe is governed, but he is not limited by the laws he has made. If he sees fit to set them aside for any particular purpose, he can do so. There is a place for miracles in God's plan.

God has a purpose to work out in and through his creation. He keeps his hand on the steering wheel of the universe. Some of his acts seem strange. His providential dealings are not always understood. But we have faith to believe that God understands, and that "to them that love God all things work together for good" (Rom. 8 : 28).

The question is often asked: "Why did God permit sin to enter his creation and why does he allow evil to continue in the world? This is one of the questions for which the finite mind of man has no definite answer, and God has not seen fit to reveal the answer. But there are three facts of which we may be sure.

First, evil cannot go beyond the permissive decrees of God. The devil could not afflict Job until he got God's permission to do so. Second, God determines the limits to which evil can go. In his affliction of Job, the devil could go only as far as God allowed. Third, God often turns that which was intended for evil into a blessing. Joseph said to his brethren, "And as for you, ye meant evil against me; but God meant it for good, to bring to pass, as it is this day, to save much people alive" (Gen. 50:20). And the psalmist said, "Surely the wrath of man shall praise thee" (Psalm 76:10).

In discussing God's providence, a few words may be said about the angels. They were created before the world, and are many in number. They are described as ministering spirits: "Are they not all ministering spirits, sent forth to do service for the sake of them that shall inherit salvation?" (Heb. 1:14). God uses the angels in working out his providential plans: "For he will give his angels charge over thee, to keep thee in all thy ways. They shall bear thee up in their hands, lest thou dash thy foot against a stone" (Psalm 91:11-12).

3. *Salvation*

Wonderful, indeed, was God's first creation, but more wonderful still is his new creation. "Wherefore if any man is in Christ, he is a new creature" (2 Cor. 5:17).

Man, whom God created in his own image, sinned against God, and fell from his high estate, bringing ruin upon himself and the whole human race. But God, in his mercy, did not leave him to his fate. He provided a way of salvation by sending his own Son into the world to redeem man from sin through his atoning death on the cross.

The whole subject of salvation will be treated in another chapter, but here we would emphasize the fact that salvation is the work of God. It was God who took the initiative in salvation; it was God who wrought out the plan of salvation; and it is God who saves by his grace. The psalmist said: "Salvation belongeth unto Jehovah" (Psalm 3:8). And Paul declared: "For by grace have ye been saved through faith; and that not of yourselves, it is the gift of God" (Eph. 2:8). And in the tenth verse of the same chapter, we have this statement: "For we are his workmanship, created in Christ Jesus."

"Oh that men would praise Jehovah for his lovingkindness, and for his wonderful works to the children of men!" (Psalm 107:8).

After nearly 2000 years of Christian history there are millions of people in the world to whom the one true God is still "the unknown God." To many others he is the neglected God. Some go so far as to say there is no God. There are two kinds of atheism; a theological atheism which denies the existence of God, and a materialistic atheism which leads men to live as if there were no God.

Many stumble because there are so many things about God which they cannot understand. God is an infinite Being, and, therefore, beyond the full comprehension of finite minds. But he is also a personal God, and willing to come into fellowship with the individual.

The story is told of a Christian lad who was asked whether his God was a big God or a little God. To which the lad replied, "He is both; he is so big that the universe cannot contain him, and so little that he can dwell in my heart."

During the War Between the States General Robert E. Lee sent his wife and daughter, Annie, to a quiet place near Warrenton, N. C., to get them out of danger. While there, Annie was stricken with fever and died. On her gravestone these words are inscribed:

> Perfect and true in all His ways,
> Whom heaven adores, and earth obeys.

3

The Crown of Creation

"And God said, Let us make man in our image" (Gen. 1:26).

MAN is the name which God gave to the highest of his creation. The Hebrew word is "Adam." This is not a proper name, like Cain and Abel, though occasionally it is so used, as in 1 Chronicles 1:1. "Adam" is a Hebrew word, which is translated by the English word "man."

Adam does not mean man as distinguished from woman; there is another word for that. It includes both man and woman. It is used in the sense of mankind. This is evident from the statement in Genesis 1:27: "And God created man in his own image, in the image of God created he him; male and female created he them."

The same truth is stated again in Genesis 5:1–2: "In the day that God created man, in the likeness of God made he him; male and female created he them, and blessed them, and called their name Adam." The root meaning of the word is red earth, probably suggestive of the fact that he was formed of the dust of the ground.

The story in Genesis reveals several truths about men.

I. THE ORIGIN OF MAN

Whence came man? To this question science gives no certain answer. Various theories have been advanced, but they are only theories, without proof. Revelation alone can give the true answer to the question, and that answer is: God created him. Three times it is declared in Genesis 1:27 that God created man.

35

1. *The Fact of Creation*

There are three accounts of the creation of man given in the Genesis story. The first one, Genesis 1 : 27, states the fact of his creation. The second, Genesis 2 : 7, reveals something of the method of his creation. The third, Genesis 2 : 21–22, gives the account of the creation of woman. The account of man's creation is repeated in Genesis 5 : 1–2.

2. *The Method of Creation*

While the fact of man's creation is stated several times, the method which God employed is not clearly given. About all we know is recorded in Genesis 2 : 7: "And Jehovah God formed man of the dust of the ground, and breathed into his nostrils the breath of life; and man became a living soul."

Two stages in the creation are implied. The first refers to his body: "And Jehovah God formed man of the dust of the ground." The body of man was fashioned from materials that were already in existence. Man's body can be analyzed, and the exact proportions of the different elements ascertained. Just how God fashioned man's body is not revealed.

The second stage in man's creation refers to his soul, or spiritual nature: "And breathed into his nostrils the breath of life; and man became a living soul." Certainly, this means more than life such as the lower animals had. To man, God imparted something of himself.

While two stages in the creation of man are suggested, we are not to think of God as collecting a pile of dust, shaping it into the form of a man, then breathing life into it.

The formation of man from the dust and the breathing of the breath of life we must not understand in a mechanical sense, as if God first of all constructed a human figure from the dust and then, by breathing His breath of life into the clod of earth which he had shaped into the form of a man, made it into a living be- ing. . . . By an act of Divine omnipotence man arose from the dust; and in the same moment in which the dust, by virtue of creative omnipotence, shaped itself into a human form, it was pervaded by the divine breath of life, and created a living being, so that we cannot say the body was earlier than the soul.[1]

Evolutionists, of course, claim that the whole creation is the result of long ages of development, and that man evolved from lower animal life. Materialistic evolutionists leave God entirely out, while other evolutionists believe that all stages of development have been under the direction of God. However, evolutionists do not agree among themselves, and the theory has raised more questions than it has answered and created more problems than it has solved. The average Christian is content with the assurance that God created man.

II. THE NATURE OF MAN

What is the nature of this creature, man, whom God created in his own image?

1. *Twofold—Body and Soul*

As indicated in the preceding discussion, man has a twofold nature—physical and spiritual. He has a body, and he has a soul.

Some Bible scholars describe man as a trinity—body, soul, and spirit. In 1 Thessalonians 5:23, Paul wrote: "And the God of peace himself sanctify you wholly; and may your spirit and soul and body be preserved entire, without blame at the coming of our Lord Jesus Christ." The author of Hebrews speaks of "the dividing of soul and spirit" (Heb. 4:12). According to this interpretation, "soul" refers to man as a living, self-conscious being, while "spirit" refers to him as a God-conscious being.

However, the two words, "soul" and "spirit," are not clearly

[1] C. F. Keil and F. Delitzsch, *Biblical Commentary on the Old Testament* (Grand Rapids: William B. Eerdmans Publishing Co., 1949), I, 79

distinguished in the Bible. Sometimes they seem to be used interchangeably. Dr. A. H. Strong says: "Man's nature is not a three-storied house, but a two-storied house, with windows in the upper story looking in two directions—toward earth and toward heaven." [2]

The account in Genesis describes man as having a twofold nature—body and soul. The two are combined to make one personality. While the soul is the most important part of a person, the body is not to be despised. It is to be respected for its true worth and dignity. The Christian's body is called the temple of the Holy Spirit: "Or know ye not that your body is a temple of the Holy Spirit which is in you, which ye have from God? and ye are not your own; for ye were bought with a price: glorify God therefore in your body" (1 Cor. 6:19–20). The body is not to be neglected, or abused, but kept clean, healthy, and strong for the service of God.

2. *In the Image of God*

Of all the creation, man alone bears the image of God: "And God said, Let us make man in our image, after our likeness" (Gen. 1:26). There seems to be no definite distinction between image and likeness. Man is a Godlike creature. In what way is he made in the image of God? Certainly, it does not mean bodily likeness, for God is Spirit, without bodily form. The likeness is in man's spiritual nature.

Dr. E. Y. Mullins suggests eight respects in which man is made in the image of God: a rational nature, a moral nature, an emotional nature, possession of will, a free being, an inclination to righteousness, dominion over the lower creation, and immortality.[3] We may sum it up under three heads.

(1) *Personality.*—Man is an intelligent, self-conscious, self-determining being. The lower animals have life but not personality. They possess certain instincts that lead them to do

[2] *Systematic Theology,* p. 246
[3] *The Christian Religion in Its Doctrinal Expression,* pp. 258–260

certain things, but they do not have the capacity to think and plan. The psalmist said: "Be ye not as the horse, or as the mule, which have no understanding" (Psalm 32:9).

Man is a free agent, with power to choose his own course. God does not force him to be righteous, neither does he restrain him when he chooses the wrong way. This right of choice is a part of the divine image in him.

It is because man is an intelligent, self-conscious, self-determining being that he is able to establish relations with his fellow man and with God. As a person, he can have fellowship with other men, and he can have fellowship with God.

(2) *Morality.*—Likeness to God means that man possesses a moral nature. He is capable of discerning between right and wrong, and he has the power to make a choice between the two. This is not true of the lower animals. They have no sense of good or evil.

Man, as God created him, was perfect in character, wholly without sin. It was after the creation of man that it was said: "And God saw everything that he had made, and, behold, it was very good" (Gen. 1:31). It was all just what God wanted it to be, including man. A perfect God could not create an imperfect being.

(3) *Immortality.*—Man, made in the image of God, is an immortal being. Since the likeness to God is not physical but spiritual, immortality does not refer to man's body but to his spirit. The body dies, but the spirit has perpetual existence. In describing death, the wise man said: "And the dust returneth to the earth as it was, and the spirit returneth unto God who gave it" (Eccl. 12:7). The body dies, but the spirit lives on.

It was because man was a rational, moral being that God gave him dominion over all his creation: "And God blessed them: and God said unto them, Be fruitful, and multiply, and replenish the earth, and subdue it; and have dominion over the fish of the sea, and over the birds of the heavens, and over every living thing that moveth upon the earth" (Gen. 1:28).

Again, in Psalm 8:4-6, we have this statement: "What is man, that thou art mindful of him? and the son of man, that thou visitest him? For thou hast made him but little lower than God, and crownest him with glory and honor. Thou makest him to have dominion over the works of thy hands; thou hast put all things under his feet."

Since man is made in the image of God, there is a dignity about human personality that must be respected. God has seen fit to bestow upon some gifts and talents greater than those bestowed on others, but that does not mean that the more privileged are to look down upon their less fortunate fellow men. All are created in the image of God, and are to be treated accordingly. There is no place for human slavery, either direct or indirect. Totalitarianism, which treats the individual as but a cog in a great machine, has no place in human relationships. Peter said he learned a great lesson down at Caesarea, namely: "That God is no respecter of persons" (Acts 10:34).

III. THE HOME OF MAN

The description of the home God prepared for man is found in Genesis 2:8-17. It was a garden of God's own planting: "And Jehovah God planted a garden eastward, in Eden; and there he put the man whom he had formed" (Gen. 2:8).

1. *Location*

Some Bible students look upon the whole creation story as an allegory. To them, the garden is but a symbol, setting forth certain truths. But the story is told in the Bible as if it represented real facts.

The garden is definitely located, "eastward, in Eden." The garden and Eden are not synonymous. Eden, meaning delight, was the country in which the garden was located. Just where that country was, is not definitely revealed. From the description given, and the rivers mentioned, it must have been somewhere in central Asia.

2. *Provision*

In that garden which God planted were beauty and plenty: "And out of the ground made Jehovah God to grow every tree that is pleasant to the sight, and good for food" (Gen. 2:9). There were two wonderful trees in the garden: the tree of life, designed to save man from death, if he had not sinned; and the tree of the knowledge of good and evil, which was to test man's loyalty to God—"But of the tree of the knowledge of good and evil, thou shalt not eat of it: for in the day that thou eatest thereof thou shalt surely die" (Gen. 2:17).

3. *Man's Occupation*

Idleness had no place in God's plan for man: "And Jehovah God took the man, and put him into the garden of Eden to dress it and to keep it" (Gen. 2:15). He was not to sit in the garden, eating its fruit and enjoying its beauty. He was to look after the garden. God never intended that man should live in idleness, either here or hereafter. In the beautiful description of the heavenly home, given in the last chapters of the Bible, the inspired writer says: "And his servants shall serve him" (Rev. 22:3).

IV. The Fall of Man

Man did not keep his first estate of sinless perfection. He disobeyed God and fell from that high and happy state. The account of his fall is given in the third chapter of Genesis.

1. *The Agent of the Fall*

The scriptural narrative gives the serpent as the agent:

"Now the serpent was more subtle than any beast of the field which Jehovah God had made. And he said unto the woman . . ." (Gen. 3:1). That the real agent in the temptation was Satan is indicated by the fact that he is later spoken of as "The old serpent, he that is called the Devil and Satan, the deceiver of the whole world" (Rev. 12:9).

Just what the appearance and characteristics of the serpent were before the fall is largely a matter of speculation. Some have pictured it as a creature of beauty, walking uprightly, instead of crawling in the dust. But the Bible does say it was the most subtle and cunning of all the creatures. It was for this reason that the devil chose the serpent as the medium of the temptation.

Who is Satan? The Bible reveals him as the chief of evil spirits, of whom there is a great number. As to their origin, we have little information. From the few passages of Scripture which reveal anything about them, we infer that they were created beings who were once without sin. Under the leadership of Satan, they rebelled against God, and were cast out from his presence.

The Scriptures speak of their fall: "And angels that kept not their own principality, but left their proper habitation . . ."(Jude 6). Peter says: "For if God spared not angels when they sinned, but cast them down to hell, and committed them to pits of darkness, to be reserved unto judgment . . ." (2 Peter 2:4). Jesus said to his disciples: "I beheld Satan fallen as lightning from heaven" (Luke 10:18). The cause of the fall of the devil and his angels is not given. Paul suggests that it may have been pride: "Not a novice, lest being puffed up he fall into the condemnation of the devil" (1 Tim. 3:6).

Thus Satan became the archenemy of God and led his hosts to oppose God in every way possible. So, when God created man, the devil sought to bring about his ruin. His methods were the same as those he uses today. He practiced deception; he covered up his real identity; he appealed to the natural appetites and desires; he created doubt as to the goodness of God; he contradicted God's word.

The devil approached the woman, who was perhaps the more trusting of the two. She yielded to the temptation and partook of the forbidden fruit. Then she persuaded Adam to join her in disobedience to God. Paul says the woman was deceived, but the man was not. He knew exactly what he was doing: "And Adam was not beguiled, but the woman being beguiled hath fallen into transgression" (1 Tim. 2:14).

The question naturally arises as to why God permitted sin to come into the world. Little is to be gained by trying to pry into the motives and purposes of God. But it may be said that man, without the opportunity to choose between right and wrong, would not have been a free agent. His would have been an enforced righteousness.

2. *The Results of the Fall*

Tragic, indeed, were the results that followed man's disobedience to God. These results were threefold.

(1) *To the man and woman.*—By their fall the man and woman marred the image of God within them and lost their fellowship with God. They were filled with fear and shame and tried to hide themselves from the presence of God. A curse was pronounced upon them:

"Unto the woman he said, I will greatly multiply thy pain and thy conception; in pain thou shalt bring forth children; and thy desire shall be to thy husband, and he shall rule over thee" (Gen. 3:16).

"And unto Adam he said, Because thou hast hearkened unto the voice of thy wife, and hast eaten of the tree, of which I commanded thee, saying, Thou shalt not eat of it: cursed is the ground for thy sake; in toil shalt thou eat of it all the days of thy life; thorns also and thistles shall it bring forth to thee; and thou shalt eat the herb of the field; in the sweat of

thy face shalt thou eat bread, till thou return unto the ground"
(Gen. 3:17–19).

The man and woman were driven out of the garden:
"Therefore Jehovah God sent him forth from the garden of
Eden, to till the ground from whence he was taken" (Gen.
3:23).

But the more terrible result of man's sin is summed up in
the word "death": "For in the day that thou eatest thereof
thou shalt surely die" (Gen. 2:17). This death was both
physical and spiritual.

From the day man disobeyed God, he was a dying creature.
His body did not die in the day he sinned, but it became
subject to disease and physical infirmities which end in death.
But man did die spiritually the day he sinned against God.
Death does not mean cessation of being, but separation, or
dissolution.

Physical death is the separation of the soul from the body.
It is described as "giving up the ghost"—"And Abraham gave
up the ghost, and died" (Gen. 25:8); "And Ananias hearing
these words fell down and gave up the ghost" (Acts 5:5).

Spiritual death is the separation of the soul from God. All
men, in their natural state, are spiritually dead. Conversion
is passing from death into life: "Verily, verily, I say unto you,
He that heareth my word, and believeth him that sent me,
hath eternal life, and cometh not into judgment, but hath
passed out of death into life" (John 5:24). More will be said
about this in the next chapter.

(2) *To the human race.*—By man's fall, he not only
brought ruin upon himself but upon all posterity. As head of
the race, Adam passed the effects of his sin on to his descendants. They became heirs of his fallen nature.

This truth is plainly stated in both the Old and New Testaments. David said: "Behold, I was brought forth in iniquity;
and in sin did my mother conceive me" (Psalm 51:5). David

was not accusing his mother of sin but was declaring that he was born with a corrupt nature. But it is in the New Testament that this truth is more clearly set forth.

In the fifth chapter of Romans, we find such statements as these: "Therefore, as through one man sin entered into the world, and death through sin; and so death passed unto all men, for that all sinned" (v. 12); "For if, by the trespass of the one, death reigned through the one" (v. 17); "So then as through one trespass the judgment came unto all men to condemnation" (v. 18); "For as through the one man's disobedience the many were made sinners" (v. 19).

In Ephesians 2:3, Paul says: "Among whom we also all once lived in the lusts of our flesh, doing the desires of the flesh and of the mind, and were by nature children of wrath, even as the rest."

Through his sin, man became corrupt in his nature. Many years later, Jesus said: "The corrupt tree bringeth forth evil fruit. A good tree cannot bring forth evil fruit, neither can a corrupt tree bring forth good fruit" (Matt. 7:17–18). A corrupt head of the race could not produce a sinless race.

This truth is not only revealed in the Scriptures, it is proved by experience. The children that were born to Adam manifested their corrupt natures. The tendency among his descendants was not toward improvement but moral deterioration, until "Jehovah saw that the wickedness of man was great in the earth, and that every imagination of the thoughts of his heart was only evil continually" (Gen. 6:5).

Future generations did not produce a single good man: "God looked down from heaven upon the children of men, to see if there were any that did understand, that did seek after God. Every one of them is gone back; they are together become filthy; there is none that doeth good, no, not one" (Psalm 53:2–3). Every child that is born into the world begins early to show signs of a sinful nature.

"Total depravity" is an expression that has been used to

describe the condition of the human race. This does not mean that man is as bad as he can be, and that no trace of good is left in him; neither does it mean that all are equally bad. Rather, it means that the whole being has been affected by sin, and that man's whole nature has been blighted by its touch.

In this connection the question naturally arises: What about babies who die in infancy, or before they reach the age of accountability? Are they lost? Some have so believed in many years gone by. It was probably this belief, that babies who died were lost unless something was done in their behalf, that led to infant baptism.

We believe that those who die before they reach the age of accountability are saved, whether they are baptized or not. They are not under condemnation until they reach the age of accountability. There is no efficacy in baptismal waters to cleanse a corrupt nature. Those who die in infancy are saved through the mercy and grace of God. David had that assurance. Concerning his little son who had died, he said: "I shall go to him, but he will not return to me" (2 Sam. 12:23).

Just when and how the little child is saved is not clearly revealed in the Scriptures. Dr. A. H. Strong makes this statement about it: "Since there is no evidence that children dying in infancy are regenerated prior to death, either with or without the use of external means, it seems most possible that the work of regeneration may be performed by the Spirit in connection with the infant soul's first view of Christ in the other world. As the remains of natural depravity in the Christian are eradicated, not by death, but at death, through the sight of Christ and union with him, so the first moment of consciousness for the infant may be coincident with a view of Christ the Savior which accomplishes the entire sanctification of its nature." [4]

[4] *Systematic Theology*, p. 357

(3) *To the rest of creation.*—There are Scripture verses which seem to indicate that the curse of man's sin fell upon all creation.

It fell upon the animal kingdom. To the serpent, God said: "Because thou hast done this, cursed art thou above all cattle, and above every beast of the field; upon thy belly shalt thou go, and dust shalt thou eat all the days of thy life" (Gen. 3:14). The whole animal kingdom was affected by the fall. Beast was arrayed against beast, tearing and destroying one another. Surely, they were not so created in the beginning.

The curse fell upon the physical creation. God said to Adam: "Because thou hast hearkened unto the voice of thy wife, and hast eaten of the tree, of which I commanded thee, saying, Thou shalt not eat of it: cursed is the ground for thy sake; in toil shalt thou eat of it all the days of thy life; thorns also and thistles shall it bring forth to thee" (Gen. 3:17–18). In Romans 8:20–22, Paul says: "For the creation was subjected to vanity, not of its own will, but by reason of him who subjected it, in hope that the creation itself also shall be delivered from the bondage of corruption into the liberty of the glory of the children of God. For we know that the whole creation groaneth and travaileth in pain together until now."

Just as the whole creation fell under the curse of sin, so it will share in the glories of redemption. In describing the glorious reign of the Messiah, Isaiah said: "And the wolf shall dwell with the lamb, and the leopard shall lie down with the kid; and the calf and the young lion and the fatling together; and a little child shall lead them. And the cow and the bear shall feed; their young ones shall lie down together; and the lion shall eat straw like the ox. And the sucking child shall play on the hole of the asp, and the weaned child shall put his hand on the adder's den. They shall not hurt nor destroy in all my holy mountain; for the earth shall be full of the knowledge of Jehovah, as the waters cover the sea" (Isa. 11:6–9).

Commenting on the foregoing passage, Dr. Alexander Maclaren says: "We cannot dogmatise on a subject of which we know so little, nor be sure of the extent to which symbolism enters into the sweet picture. Enough that there surely comes a time when the King of men and Lord of nature shall bring back peace between both, and restore 'the fair music that all creatures made To their great Lord.'" [5]

John, in telling of one of the wonderful visions he had, said: "And every created thing which is in the heaven, and on the earth, and under the earth, and on the sea, and all things that are in them, heard I saying, Unto him that sitteth on the throne, and unto the Lamb, be the blessing, and the honor, and the glory, and the dominion, for ever and ever" (Rev. 5:13).

But, as Dr. Maclaren reminds us: "We cannot dogmatise on a subject of which we know so little."

We can sing with Isaac Watts:

> Let all on earth their voices raise,
> To sing the great Jehovah's praise,
>   And bless his holy name:
> His glory let the people know,
> His wonders to the nations show,
>   His saving grace proclaim.
>
> He framed the globe; He built the sky;
> He made the shining worlds on high,
>   And reigns in glory there:
> His beams are majesty and light;
> His beauties, how divinely bright!
>   His dwelling place, how fair!
>
> Come the great day, the glorious hour,
> When earth shall feel His saving power,
>   All nations fear His name;
> Then shall the race of men confess
> The beauty of His holiness,
>   His saving grace proclaim.

[5] *Expositions on the Book of Isaiah*, pp. 62–63

4

The Sinfulness of Sin

"That through the commandment sin might become exceeding sinful" (Rom. 7:13).

SEVERAL different words are used in the Bible to designate the breach between God and man. It is called transgression, iniquity, wickedness, offense, disobedience, and lawlessness. But the word which is most commonly used to describe man's failure is "sin." This is the word which God himself used. In his warning to Cain, he said: "If thou doest not well, sin coucheth at the door" (Gen. 4:7).

The root meaning of the word which is translated "sin" is missing the mark, or falling short. Sin is falling short of the goal which God has placed before us; it is missing the mark which God has set up. Paul expressed it in Romans 3:23: "For all have sinned, and fall short of the glory of God." They have not measured up to what God intended they should be.

I. THE AUTHOR OF SIN

Something of the beginning of sin was mentioned in the preceding chapter. All we know about it is recorded in the first seven verses of the third chapter of Genesis. While the name of Satan does not appear in the story, it is evident that he was the real author of sin. The story reveals some of the methods he used in the beginning, and has continued to use.

1. *Concealed His Own Identity*

"Now the serpent was more subtle than any beast of the field which Jehovah God had made" (Gen. 3:1). This is the

49

reason Satan selected the serpent above all other animals—
he was the most cunning of all.

Satan has many disguises behind which he hides. He never
comes to a person and introduces himself by saying, "I am
the devil." Paul says he sometimes appears as an angel of
light: "For even Satan fashioneth himself into an angel of
light" (2 Cor. 11:14).

2. *Raised a Doubt as to the Love of God*

"And he said unto the woman, Yea, hath God said, Ye shall
not eat of any tree of the garden?" (Gen. 3:1); "For God
doth know that in the day ye eat thereof, then your eyes shall
be opened, and ye shall be as God, knowing good and evil"
(Gen. 3:5). He implied that God was holding back from
them something which they should have.

3. *Contradicted God's Word*

"And the serpent said unto the woman, Ye shall not surely
die" (Gen. 3:4). The devil has won a great victory when he
can lead one to doubt the truth of God's word. God says:
"The soul that sinneth, it shall die" (Ezek. 18:4); the devil
says: "Ye shall not surely die." God says: "The wages of sin is
death" (Rom. 6:23); the devil says: "Ye shall not surely die."

4. *Appealed to the Woman's Natural Desires*

"And when the woman saw that the tree was good for food,
and that it was a delight to the eyes, and that the tree was to
be desired to make one wise, she took of the fruit thereof, and
did eat" (Gen. 3:6). Many years later, John wrote about
"the lust of the flesh and the lust of the eyes and the vain-
glory of life" (1 John 2:16). We are reminded of the three
temptations which the devil brought to our Lord.

5. *Worked Through the Woman to Win the Man*

"And she gave also unto her husband with her, and he did

eat" (Gen. 3:6). Jesus says to those who surrender their lives to him: "Ye shall be my witnesses" (Acts 1:8); and the devil says to those who yield their lives unto him: "Ye shall be my witnesses." The devil has more witnesses in the world than the Lord, and many times they are far more zealous than the witnesses of Christ.

II. The Nature of Sin

There are various concepts of sin in the world. Some deny the existence of sin, but denying its existence does not destroy it. God has some very emphatic things to say about this attitude: "If we say that we have no sin, we deceive ourselves, and the truth is not in us" (1 John 1:8); "If we say that we have not sinned, we make him a liar, and his word is not in us" (1 John 1:10).

Some people laugh at sin. God characterizes such people as fools: "Fools make a mock at sin" (Prov. 14:9 KJV). Surely, there is nothing in all the world so foolish as to make a joke of sin.

There are those who boast of their sins. Isaiah, in describing the sins of Jerusalem and Judah, said: "The show of their countenance doth witness against them; and they declare their sin as Sodom, they hide it not" (Isa. 3:9). There is an old saying: "He that falls into sin is a man; he that grieves at sin is a saint; he that boasts of sin is a devil."

But perhaps the most dangerous attitude toward sin is that which would tone it down so that it does not appear to be so bad. It is called by different names, such as maladjustment, moral lapse, or even disease, for which men are not responsible. But changing the name of a thing does not change its character.

Dr. Chapman used to tell of a minister who preached an earnest sermon on sin. One of the officers of the church went to him later and said: "We do not want you to talk so plainly about sin, because if our boys and girls hear you talking so much about it, they will more easily become sinners. Call it a mistake, if you will, but do not speak so plainly about sin."

The pastor took a small bottle of strychnine marked "Poison," and showed it to the visitor, saying: "I see what you want me to do. You want me to change the label. Now suppose I take this label off and substitute another, say, 'Essence of Peppermint.' Do you see what will happen? The milder you make the label, the more dangerous you make the poison." Whatever name may be given to sin, it is still the abominable thing which God hates.

We are accustomed to describe sin as something black. We speak of the black crimes that are committed. But that is not the word which God uses to describe sin. He calls it red, or scarlet: "Come now, and let us reason together, saith Jehovah: though your sins be as scarlet, they shall be as white as snow; though they be red like crimson, they shall be as wool" (Isa. 1:18).

An expert in the field of dyeing cloth gave this testimony. He said they could change cloth from one color to another without much trouble, except in the case of red. Black could be changed into another color very easily. But not so with red. They could change that for a little while, but, sooner or later, the crimson hue would appear.

God describes sin, not as black, but as red. It is deep-dyed and hard to change. The only thing in all the world that will wash it out is the blood of Christ: "The blood of Jesus his Son cleanseth us from all sin" (1 John 1:7).

It seems that Paul could find no word which he considered strong enough to describe the terrible nature of sin. After searching for such a word all through the vocabulary, the only thing he could say about it was that sin was "exceeding sinful." And he was not describing any particular sin. He did not point out some heinous crime, and say: "That is exceeding sinful." All sin, any sin, is exceeding sinful. That does not mean that some sins are not greater than others. Certainly they are. But Paul was trying to emphasize the truth that all sin is terrible in its nature.

1. *Rebellion Against God*

We speak of sinning against our fellow men, and so we do. But all sin is against God. John says: "Sin is lawlessness" (1 John 3:4). The King James Version has it: "Sin is the transgression of the law." Whose law? Not the law of men. We do not speak of the transgression of human law as sin. We have other words for that, such as misdemeanor, felony, crime, etc. The word "sin" is reserved for the transgression of God's law.

That is what makes sin so terrible—it is against a holy and loving God. It was the realization of this truth that broke David's heart. When he was brought under conviction for his great sin, he cried out: "I have sinned against Jehovah" (2 Sam. 12:13). To be sure, he had sinned against Uriah, and against Uriah's wife, but the thing that made it so terrible was that he had sinned against God. So deeply was this truth burned into his heart that, in his prayer of penitence, he said: "Against thee, thee only, have I sinned, and done that which is evil in thy sight" (Psalm 51:4).

The devil led the first man and woman into sin, not because he cared whether they were saved or lost. His primary purpose was, through their sin, to make a thrust at God. That is his primary purpose in all sin. He is not primarily interested in whether you and I are saved or lost. His one great purpose is to lead us into sin that he may use us in his fight against God. That is what sin means—we have put ourselves in Satan's hands that he may use us to make a thrust at the heart of God.

In order to get some conception of the true nature of sin, we must go to the cross of Calvary. Sin is the thing that crucified the Son of God. It was sin that took the whip and beat his back until it bled; it was sin that plaited the crown of thorns and pressed it on his brow; it was sin that took the hammer and drove the nails into his hands and feet; it was the thing we call sin that nailed the Son of God to the cross.

Whose sin crucified Jesus Christ? Someone will say: "It was the sin of Judas Iscariot, who betrayed him into the hands of his enemies"; or: "It was the sin of the Jewish rulers who condemned him to death"; or: "It was the sin of Pontius Pilate, who delivered him into the hands of Roman soldiers"; or: "It was the sin of the Roman soldiers, who nailed him to the cross." It is true that the sin of all these had part in the crucifixion of the Son of God, but they were not alone in their guilt.

It was the world's sin that crucified Jesus Christ. Your sin and mine had part in it. With us, the cross is an event in history; but with God, it is an eternal transaction.

The Scriptures speak of crucifying the Son of God afresh: "Seeing they crucify to themselves the Son of God afresh, and put him to an open shame" (Heb. 6:6). That is what men do when they turn away from the love of God in Christ, and give themselves to sin. They are saying, in act if not in word: "Let me have the whip that I may beat his back; let me have the crown of thorns that I may press it on his brow; let me have the hammer that I may drive the nails into his hands and feet."

2. *Universal in Its Reach*

The testimony of Scripture, in both the Old and New Testaments is that sin is universal. Solomon said: "For there is no man that sinneth not" (1 Kings 8:46). The psalmist declared: "There is none that doeth good, no, not one" (Psalm 53:3). John used this strong language: "If we say that we have not sinned, we make him a liar, and his word is not in us" (1 John 1:10). And Paul summed it up in these words: "For all have sinned, and fall short of the glory of God" (Rom. 3:23).

"All" is a little word, but it embraces a multitude of people. It reaches back to the beginning of time and takes in all the generations that have lived on earth. It reaches across seas and continents and includes every human being in the world today. It reaches on down to the end of time and takes in all the generations that are yet to be.

This is not only the witness of the Bible, it is the testimony of human experience. A perfectly righteous man or woman has never been found. Those who have reached the highest heights in Christian experience are most ready to admit their failures and shortcomings. All have not sinned alike. Some have gone deeper into sin than others, but there is no one who has not sinned.

Some do not class themselves as sinners because they have not been guilty of the gross sins of society. They are not drunkards, or thieves, or adulterers, or criminals. But they may be guilty of other sins that are just as bad in the sight of God. This was the mistake the Pharisee in the Temple made: "God, I thank thee, that I am not as the rest of men, extortioners, unjust, adulterers" (Luke 18:11).

The Pharisee thought, because he was not guilty of these gross sins, he was not a sinner. But he was guilty of hypocrisy, which is one of the worst of all sins in the sight of God. Jesus never showed his righteous indignation more than when he was talking to hypocrites: "Woe unto you, scribes and Pharisees, hypocrites!" (Matt. 23:15).

Unbelief is held up in the Scriptures as the major sin. In speaking of the coming of the Holy Spirit, Jesus said: "And he, when he is come, will convict the world in respect of sin, and of righteousness, and of judgment: of sin, because they believe not on me" (John 16:8–9). The author of Hebrews sounds warning: "Take heed, brethren, lest haply there shall be in any one of you an evil heart of unbelief" (Heb. 3:12). Jesus did not say: "He will convict the world in respect of sin, because they are drunkards, murderers, adulterers," etc., but "because they believe not on me." The author of Hebrews did not say: "Lest there be in any of you an evil heart of murder, adultery," or other sins, but "an evil heart of unbelief."

Some years ago, as reported in the *Sunday School Times,* Dr. Eugene Lyman Fisk, medical examiner of the Life Extension Institute, made this statement: "There is something wrong with all of us physically. Physical perfection is still the most elusive thing in the world. We have given up hope of finding physical perfection, and I might go as far as to say, it is no longer attainable. I have found among the men I have examined, not one grade *A* man. Even the grade *B*'s are all too rare. It is even impossible to find a perfect specimen at birth."

If that be true of man's physical being, how much more is it true of his moral nature. There are no perfect specimens. The Great Physician "looked down from heaven upon the children of men, to see if there were any that did understand, that did seek after God." The verdict was: "Every one of them is gone back; they are together become filthy; there is none that doeth good, no, not one" (Psalm 53:2–3).

3. *The Unpardonable Sin*

The Bible speaks of a sin for which there is no pardon. Jesus said: "Therefore I say unto you, Every sin and blasphemy shall be forgiven unto men; but the blasphemy against the Spirit shall not be forgiven. And whosoever shall speak a word against the Son of man, it shall be forgiven him; but whosoever shall speak against the Holy Spirit, it shall not be forgiven him, neither in this world, nor in that which is to come" (Matt. 12:31–32).

In Hebrews 10:26 we have this statement: "For if we sin

wilfully after that we have received the knowledge of the truth, there remaineth no more a sacrifice for sins." And in 1 John 5:16, we read: "If any man see his brother sinning a sin not unto death, he shall ask, and God will give him life for them that sin not unto death. There is a sin unto death: not concerning this do I say that he should make request."

Since Jesus said there is only one sin for which there is no pardon, these passages must refer to the same thing. The sin mentioned in these verses is unpardonable, not because God is not willing to pardon, but because the one who has committed it has hardened himself against God until there is no longer any response to divine influences. The fear which some have that they have committed this sin is evidence that they have not. For when one is guilty of this sin, there is no more feeling about it. It is like cement that gradually hardens until it becomes set.

What is this unpardonable sin? The Scriptures have not revealed a great deal about it. The sin which Jesus condemned in the Pharisees was that of ascribing the miracles of Christ, wrought in the power of the Holy Spirit, to Satan. But this was the culmination of a long season of hardening their hearts against Christ. Finally, they consciously, and wilfully, and maliciously, rejected him. It would seem, then, from this and other passages of Scripture, that the unpardonable sin is a long course of hardening the heart against divine influence, culminating in an act of wilful and final rejection.

Dr. J. P. Thompson, quoted by Dr. A. H. Strong, gives this definition of the unpardonable sin: "The unpardonable sin is the knowing, wilful, persistent, contemptuous, malignant spurning of divine truth and grace, as manifested to the soul by the convincing and illuminating power of the Holy Ghost." [1]

[1] *Systematic Theology,* p. 350

III. The Consequences of Sin

The consequences of sin are both immediate and remote, both physical and spiritual. Sin brought immediate consequences in the case of Adam and Eve. They became subject to sorrow, and suffering, and death. They were driven from the garden and alienated from God.

There are some sins that still bring immediate consequences. There are many people who are suffering in mind and body because of their sins. There are those who are spending their lives behind iron bars because of their sins. Many have gone down to untimely graves because of their sins. It may be said that all the sorrow and suffering in the world is the direct, or indirect, result of sin; for if there had been no sin, these things would not be.

The one word which best describes the consequences of sin is "death." Sin is the transgression of God's law. Law which carries no penalty for its violation is worthless. Legislatures may meet and pass laws, but, if there is no penalty for the breach of those laws, wicked men will trample them under foot and laugh in the face of those who made them. God's law must carry a penalty for its violation. If not, men would break it and laugh in the face of God.

God's law carries the death penalty. To Adam and Eve he said: "In the day that thou eatest thereof thou shalt surely die" (Gen. 2:17). The prophet Ezekiel, speaking for God, said: "The soul that sinneth, it shall die" (Ezek. 18:4). James, the brother of our Lord, said: "And the sin, when it is fullgrown, bringeth forth death" (James 1:15). And Paul sums it up in these words: "The wages of sin is death" (Rom. 6:23).

Sometimes, in periods of depression, wages have to be reduced. But the wages of sin have never been reduced. That wage scale was set in the beginning of creation, and has never been changed.

There are two kinds of death, and both of them are the results of sin.

1. *Physical Death*

The death of the body is a part of the penalty of sin. If there had been no sin, there would have been no physical death. God had made wonderful provision by which Adam and Eve might have escaped death, if they had not sinned. He placed in the garden the tree of life, whose fruit they might have eaten, and lived forever. Whether this is to be taken as figurative or literal language, the truth is the same. God had provided a way whereby they might have escaped death.

The Scriptures say Adam and Eve were driven from the garden, not because they had sinned, but to prevent them from taking of the tree of life: "And Jehovah God said, Behold, the man is become as one of us, to know good and evil; and now, lest he put forth his hand, and take also of the tree of life, and eat, and live for ever—therefore Jehovah God sent him forth from the garden of Eden, to till the ground from whence he was taken. So he drove out the man; and he placed at the east of the garden of Eden the Cherubim, and the flame of a sword which turned every way, to keep the way of the tree of life" (Gen. 3:22–24).

From that day to this, death has reigned in the world. All who have lived in earth have died, with two miraculous exceptions, Enoch and Elijah. The whole earth has become one great graveyard. In some cases death is the direct result of definite sin, or sins; but all death is the indirect result of sin in the human race.

2. *Spiritual Death*

The essential meaning of death is not extinction but separation, with its accompanying ruin. Physical death means the separation of the soul and body, resulting in the decay of the body. The body returns to the dust, and the spirit returns to God. In describing death, the wise man said: "And the dust returneth to the earth as it was, and the spirit returneth unto God who gave it" (Eccl. 12:7). Spiritual death is separation of the soul from God, resulting in the ruin of the soul.

In his natural state, man is spiritually dead, alienated from God. Paul described the spiritual condition of the Ephesians, before their conversion, as "dead through your trespasses and sins," and "by nature children of wrath" (Eph. 2:1, 3). They were alienated from God, "being darkened in their understanding, alienated from the life of God, because of the ignorance that is in them, because of the hardening of their heart" (Eph. 4:18).

This spiritual death culminates in eternal death, eternal separation from God, eternal ruin of the soul, unless one comes to know God: "Them that know not God ... shall suffer punishment, even eternal destruction from the face of the Lord and from the glory of his might" (2 Thess. 1:8–9).

This eternal ruin of the soul is spoken of as the second death: "Blessed and holy is he that hath part in the first resurrection: over these the second death hath no power" (Rev. 20:6); "But for the fearful, and unbelieving, and abominable, and murderers, and fornicators, and sorcerers, and idolaters, and all liars, their part shall be in the lake that burneth with fire and brimstone; which is the second death" (Rev. 21:8).

There is a first death and a second death, just as there is a first birth and a second birth. There is a physical birth and a spiritual birth—the birth of the body and the rebirth of the soul. In like manner, there is a first death and a second death—the death of the body and the death of the soul. Both are the wages of sin. And, just as the spiritual birth is more glorious than the physical birth, so the spiritual death is more terrible than the physical death.

5

The Saviour of Men

"Thou shalt call his name Jesus; for it is he that shall save his people from their sins" (Matt. 1:21).

When Adam sinned, and thus brought ruin on himself, and upon the whole human race, three courses were open to God—to condemn all mankind without mercy, to save all mankind, or to offer a way of salvation to those who would repent and turn to God. The latter was the only course for a just and loving God. Accordingly, he promised a Messiah, who would save his people from their sins.

There was a promise of the Messiah in the curse pronounced upon the serpent: "And I will put enmity between thee and the woman, and between thy seed and her seed: he shall bruise thy head, and thou shalt bruise his heel" (Gen. 3:15). This promise was repeated many times in the centuries that·followed. Men looked forward in hope and trust to the coming of that Saviour.

In the fulness of time the Saviour came: "But when the fulness of the time came, God sent forth his Son, born of a woman, born under the law, that he might redeem them that were under the law, that we might receive the adoption of sons" (Gal. 4:4–5).

The personal name which God gave to his Son was Jesus —"Thou shalt call his name Jesus." This is equivalent to the Hebrew "Joshua," which means, Jehovah is salvation. The official title given to Jesus was "Christ," which means Anointed. It is the Greek equivalent of the Hebrew "Messiah." This designated Jesus as the one who fulfilled all the messianic hopes. In the Epistles, the personal name and the official title are usually combined—Jesus Christ, or Christ Jesus.

Still another title given to Jesus was "Lord." This was a title of dignity, and honor, and majesty. The word, as used in the New Testament, almost invariably refers to Jesus. Sometimes he is called "Lord Jesus," and sometimes all three titles are combined, "the Lord Jesus Christ."

I. THE PRE-EXISTENCE OF CHRIST

The existence of Christ did not, as in the case of ordinary men, begin with his birth. He existed in an eternal past.

1. *Clearly Stated in the New Testament*

Only a few passages need to be quoted here. We begin with John 1:1-2: "In the beginning was the Word, and the Word was with God, and the Word was God. The same was in the beginning with God." The same words are used here that we find in the first verse of the Bible, "In the beginning." Before the creation of the world, Christ existed with the Father.

John goes on to say that Christ was the agent of the creation: "All things were made through him; and without him was not anything made that hath been made" (John 1:3).

Paul states the same truth in Colossians 1:16: "For in him were all things created, in the heavens and upon the earth, things visible and things invisible, whether thrones or dominions or principalities or powers; all things have been created through him, and unto him." And in verse 17, he continues—"And he is before all things, and in him all things consist."

2. *Pre-existence Claimed by Jesus*

More than once Jesus spoke of his existence in an eternal past. To the unbelieving Jews he said: "Verily, verily, I say unto you, Before Abraham was born, I am" (John 8:58). Abraham lived nearly two thousand years before Jesus was born, and yet he said: "Before Abraham was born, I am." In his intercessory prayer, he said: "And now, Father, glorify thou me with thine own self with the glory which I had with thee before the world was" (John 17:5).

II. THE INCARNATION OF CHRIST

By incarnation is meant taking a body of flesh. The eternal Son of God came to earth and clothed himself in a human body: "And the Word became flesh, and dwelt among us" (John 1:14). Paul stated it in this manner: "Who, existing in the form of God, counted not the being on an equality with God a thing to be grasped, but emptied himself, taking the form of a servant, being made in the likeness of men" (Phil. 2:6–7). This is what happened when the Babe was born in Bethlehem.

Two truths are involved in the incarnation of Christ.

1. *Truly Man*

The name by which Jesus spoke of himself more often than any other was "Son of man." The whole gospel story presents him as a man. He lived like a man and manifested the traits of a man. He grew in physical stature: "And Jesus advanced in wisdom and stature, and in favor with God and men" (Luke 2:52). Jesus got tired and hungry: "Jesus therefore, being wearied with his journey, sat thus by the well" (John 4:6); "And when he had fasted forty days and forty nights, he afterward hungered" (Matt. 4:2). He suffered physical pain, he wept, he went to sleep, he died. All of these experiences bear witness to the humanity of Jesus.

2. *Truly God*

Jesus was not only the Son of man, he was the Son of God.

He claimed deity for himself: "He that hath seen me hath seen the Father" (John 14:9); "I and the Father are one" (John 10:30). He exercised the power of God. He forgave sin: "And Jesus seeing their faith saith unto the sick of the palsy, Son, thy sins are forgiven" (Mark 2:5). His enemies condemned him to death because he claimed to be the Son of God: "The Jews answered him, We have a law, and by that law he ought to die, because he made himself the Son of God" (John 19:7).

So, in Christ we have the God-man, two natures combined in one person. He was so much man that he hungered; he was so much God that he fed the hungry multitude with five barley loaves and two small fishes. He was so much man that he grew tired; he was so much God that he gave rest to the weary. He was so much man that he fell asleep; he was so much God that he awoke and rebuked the storm. He was so much man that he died; he was so much God that he arose from the dead. It was only as the God-man that he could be the Saviour of the world.

Do we understand this? Of course not. And because some people cannot understand it, they refuse to accept it as truth. Daniel Webster was asked one day, "Do you understand Jesus Christ?" To which he replied: "No, I would be ashamed to acknowledge him as my Saviour if I could understand him. I need a superhuman Saviour—one so great and so glorious that I cannot understand him."

III. The Deity of Christ

What has been said raises the question of the deity of Christ. There is a difference between divinity and deity, as the words are used today. There is a sense in which all men can claim to be divine, in that they are created in the image of God. There is a Godlikeness in them. But no mere man can claim deity for himself. That is a distinction that belongs

to Jesus, the Man of Galilee. The Bishop of Durham is quoted
as having said: "A Christ who is not God is a bridge broken
at the farther end."

1. *The Nature of His Birth*

There was never birth like the birth of the Babe in Bethlehem. Matthew says: "Now the birth of Jesus Christ was on
this wise: When his mother Mary had been betrothed to
Joseph, before they came together she was found with child
of the Holy Spirit. And Joseph her husband, being a righteous man, and not willing to make her a public example,
was minded to put her away privily. But when he thought
on these things, behold, an angel of the Lord appeared unto
him in a dream, saying, Joseph, thou son of David, fear not
to take unto thee Mary thy wife: for that which is conceived
in her is of the Holy Spirit" (Matt. 1:18–20).

Luke corroborates the story of Matthew and makes it even
stronger: "Now in the sixth month the angel Gabriel was
sent from God unto a city of Galilee, named Nazareth, to a
virgin betrothed to a man whose name was Joseph, of the
house of David; and the virgin's name was Mary. And he
came in unto her, and said, Hail, thou that art highly favored,
the Lord is with thee. But she was greatly troubled at the
saying, and cast in her mind what manner of salutation this
might be. And the angel said unto her, Fear not, Mary: for
thou hast found favor with God. And behold, thou shalt conceive in thy womb, and bring forth a son, and shalt call his
name Jesus" (Luke 1:26–31). Then, in verse 35, Luke explains the manner of Jesus' birth in these words: "And the
angel answered and said unto her, The Holy Spirit shall
come upon thee, and the power of the Most High shall over-
shadow thee: wherefore also the holy thing which is begotten
shall be called the Son of God."

Those who deny the virgin birth of Jesus are denying the
truth of God's Word.

2. *The Manner of His Life*

Jesus lived a perfect life. The author of Hebrews says of him: "One that hath been in all points tempted like as we are, yet without sin" (Heb. 4:15). Jesus could stand before his enemies and challenge them to name a single sin of which he was guilty: "Which of you convicteth me of sin?" (John 8:46). The statement of Pilate is the verdict of the ages: "I find no fault in this man" (Luke 23:4). Romanes said of him: "The most extraordinary thing about Jesus is the fact that twenty centuries have failed to find a fault in him." None but the Son of God could live like that.

3. *The Character of His Teachings*

When men were sent from Jerusalem to seize Jesus and bring him before the Sanhedrin, they returned without him. When questioned concerning their failure, they replied: "Never man so spake" (John 7:46).

Never man spoke like this man because there was never a man like that man. There have been silver-tongued orators who swayed the multitudes with their eloquence, there have been great scholars who startled men with their learning; but never man spake like Jesus. His words were both simple and profound. The common people heard him gladly, and the wisest of men marveled at his words. The principles he set forth have been the guiding light of the centuries.

4. *The Wonder of His Works*

When Nicodemus, the Jewish ruler, came to Jesus by night, he said to him: "Rabbi, we know that thou art a teacher come from God; for no one can do these signs that thou doest, except God be with him" (John 3:2). That is the explanation which Jesus himself gave of his miracles. Standing before the multitude in Jerusalem, he said: "But the witness which I have is greater than that of John; for the works which the Father hath given me to accomplish, the very works that I do, bear witness of me, that the Father hath sent me" (John 5:36).

5. *The Glory of His Resurrection*

Paul declared that the resurrection of Jesus was the sure proof of his deity: "Concerning his Son, who was born of the seed of David according to the flesh, who was declared to be the Son of God with power, according to the Spirit of holiness, by the resurrection from the dead; even Jesus Christ our Lord" (Rom. 1:3–4). He was nailed to a cross and left to hang there and die. His dead body was taken from the cross and laid in a rock-hewn tomb.

A great stone was rolled across the mouth of the tomb and sealed with the Roman seal. To make sure that dead body was not disturbed, a guard of Roman soldiers was set to watch it. But, on the third day, that dead body came out of the tomb and lived again in glorified form. That, says Paul, is the sure proof of the deity of Christ.

IV. THE DEATH OF CHRIST

The crucifixion of Jesus was the greatest crime of the ages. And yet it was the supreme manifestation of the love of God: "But God commendeth his own love toward us, in that, while we were yet sinners, Christ died for us" (Rom. 5:8). This is the finest of all illustrations of how God changes curses into blessings. Joseph said to his brethren: "And as for you, ye meant evil against me; but God meant it for good, to bring to pass, as it is this day, to save much people alive" (Gen. 50:20). The enemies of Christ thought to make the crucifixion their greatest victory, but God turned it into their greatest defeat. Through the cross he wrought out salvation for a lost world.

There are several important truths associated with the death of Christ.

1. *Voluntary*

Jesus did not go to the cross because he was helpless in the hands of his enemies. When Peter drew his sword to defend his Master in the garden of Gethsemane, Jesus said to him: "Put up again thy sword into its place: for all they that take the sword shall perish with the sword. Or thinkest thou that I cannot beseech my Father, and he shall even now send me more than twelve legions of angels?" (Matt. 26:52-53).

Not all the schemes of Jewish rulers, not all the authority of Roman governors, not all the power of Roman arms, could have nailed Jesus to the cross. Concerning his death, Jesus said: "I lay down my life, that I may take it again. No one taketh it away from me, but I lay it down of myself" (John 10:17-18). He declared that he came to the world to die: "Even as the Son of man came not to be ministered unto, but to minister, and to give his life a ransom for many" (Matt. 20:28).

2. *Substitutionary*

It was not the manner of Christ's death that was important, but the meaning of it. Others have been crucified. In his death, Christ opened up a way of salvation for sinful men.

The Word of God says, "The wages of sin is death" (Rom. 6:23). It further declares that all are guilty before God: "For all have sinned, and fall short of the glory of God" (Rom. 3:23). How, then, could God save anybody, and maintain his own righteousness, and uphold his law?

The cross of Christ is the answer to that question: "Being justified freely by his grace through the redemption that is in Christ Jesus: whom God set forth to be a propitiation, through faith, in his blood, to show his righteousness because of the passing over of the sins done aforetime, in the forbearance of God; for the showing, I say, of his righteousness at this present season: that he might himself be just, and the justifier of him that hath faith in Jesus" (Rom. 3:24–26).

There have been many theories of the atonement suggested, but the plain teaching of the Bible is that the death of Jesus was substitutionary. He took man's place before the broken law of God and suffered in his stead. This was foretold in the Old Testament Scriptures.

God pulled back the curtain and permitted Isaiah to look seven centuries into the future and catch a vision of Calvary's cross. This is what he saw: "He was wounded for our transgressions, he was bruised for our iniquities; the chastisement of our peace was upon him; and with his stripes we are healed. All we like sheep have gone astray; we have turned every one to his own way; and Jehovah hath laid on him the iniquity of us all" (Isa. 53:5–6).

The substitutionary death of Christ is plainly stated in the New Testament. There is no other logical explanation of such passages as the following:

"Him who knew no sin he made to be sin on our behalf; that we might become the righteousness of God in him" (2 Cor. 5:21).

"Christ redeemed us from the curse of the law, having become a curse for us" (Gal. 3:13).

"Who his own self bare our sins in his body upon the tree, that we, having died unto sins, might live unto righteousness; by whose stripes ye were healed" (1 Peter 2:24).

"That by the grace of God he should taste of death for every man" (Heb. 2:9).

"And he is the propitiation for our sins; and not for ours only, but also for the whole world" (1 John 2:2). Jesus carried the world in his heart when he went to the cross.

3. *Once for All*

There will never be another Saviour, because the world will never need another. Christ is sufficient for all men, for all time. There will never be another Calvary, for the atonement wrought out there meets the needs of sinful men everywhere. Christ died once for all: "But now once at the end of the ages hath he been manifested to put away sin by the sacrifice of himself." . . . "So Christ also, having been once offered to bear the sins of many" (Heb. 9:26, 28).

> Dear dying Lamb, Thy precious blood
> Shall never lose its power,
> Till all the ransomed Church of God
> Be saved, to sin no more.
>
> WILLIAM COWPER

V. THE RESURRECTION OF CHRIST

Christ died on the cross, and was buried in Joseph's tomb, but he is not dead today. On the third day he arose from the grave, and is alive forevermore.

This is one of the distinguishing marks of the Christian religion that sets it apart from all other religions. We have a living Saviour. Buddha lived several centuries before Christ. He established his religious system, and, in a few years, he died. And he is dead today. His body still sleeps in the earth. Mohammed lived several centuries after Christ. He, too, established a religion, and he died. He, too, is still dead. In that Eastern grave his body lies.

Christ died, but he is not dead today. Roman seals and Roman guards could not keep his body in the tomb. He broke the bonds of death and came forth to live forevermore —"Knowing that Christ being raised from the dead dieth no more; death no more hath dominion over him" (Rom. 6:9).

There is no fact in history more clearly proved than the resurrection of Christ. The empty grave, the grave clothes, the testimony of faithful witnesses, and many other well-established facts, prove that Jesus arose from the dead. His influence in the world today proves that he is alive.

A devout Christian man was asked by an unbeliever why he believed that Christ rose from the dead. The old man replied: "Well, one reason is that I was talking with him for half an hour this morning."

There are some precious truths associated with the resurrection of Christ.

1. Completed the Work of the Cross

A dead Christ could not be a Saviour. His resurrection gave assurance that God had accepted his atoning work on the cross—"Who was delivered up for our trespasses, and was raised for our justification" (Rom. 4:25). Paul said: "If Christ hath not been raised, your faith is vain; ye are yet in your sins" (1 Cor. 15:17).

The death and resurrection of Christ constituted the heart of the gospel which Paul preached: "Now I make known unto you, brethren, the gospel which I preached unto you, which also ye received, wherein also ye stand, by which also ye are saved, if ye hold fast the word which I preached unto you, except ye believed in vain. For I delivered unto you first of all that which also I received: that Christ died for our sins according to the scriptures; and that he was buried; and that he hath been raised on the third day according to the scriptures" (1 Cor. 15:1-4).

2. Furnishes Proof of Life Beyond the Grave

All through the ages men sought some tangible proof of immortality. Job cried out: "If a man die, shall he live again?" (Job 14:14). The resurrection of Christ was the answer to that age-long cry.

Paul said: "Who saved us, and called us with a holy calling, not according to our works, but according to his own purpose and grace, which was given us in Christ Jesus before times eternal, but hath now been manifested by the appearing of our Saviour Christ Jesus, who abolished death, and brought life and immortality to light through the gospel" (2 Tim. 1:9–10).

The resurrection of Christ declares that death is not the end of the story. There is life beyond the grave.

3. *Gave the Promise and Pattern of the Resurrection of Christ's People*

In 1 Corinthians 15:20, we have this statement from the pen of Paul: "But now hath Christ been raised from the dead, the firstfruits of them that are asleep."

The first fruits which were offered unto the Lord were the promise and sample of the coming harvest. In offering their first fruits, the people were expressing their assurance that, by the blessing of God, there would be a harvesttime, and these first fruits were a sample of what the harvest would be. So the resurrection of Christ is the assurance of the resurrection of the dead: "For as in Adam all die, so also in Christ shall all be made alive. But each in his own order: Christ the firstfruits; then they that are Christ's, at his coming" (1 Cor. 15:22–23). "O death, where is thy sting? O grave, where is thy victory?" (1 Cor. 15:55 KJV).

The resurrection of Christ gave the pattern of what the resurrection body will be: "For our citizenship is in heaven; whence also we wait for a Saviour, the Lord Jesus Christ: who shall fashion anew the body of our humiliation, that it may be conformed to the body of his glory" (Phil. 3:20–21). And John says: "Beloved, now are we children of God, and it is not yet made manifest what we shall be. We know that, if he shall be manifested, we shall be like him; for we shall see him even as he is" (1 John 3:2).

VI. The Exaltation of Christ

Following his resurrection, Christ remained on earth forty days, appearing from time to time to his disciples. Then he ascended to heaven and took his place at the right hand of God.

Luke, in the closing verses of his Gospel, gives an account of the ascension of the risen Lord: "And he led them out until they were over against Bethany: and he lifted up his hands, and blessed them. And it came to pass, while he blessed them, he parted from them, and was carried up into heaven" (Luke 24 : 50–51).

In the first chapter of Acts, Luke takes up where his Gospel closed, and gives again the story of the ascension: "And when he had said these things, as they were looking, he was taken up; and a cloud received him out of their sight" (Acts 1:9).

Other Scripture passages tell us something of what took place on the other side of that cloud: "Wherefore also God highly exalted him, and gave unto him the name which is above every name; that in the name of Jesus every knee should bow, of things in heaven and things on earth and things under the earth, and that every tongue should confess that Jesus Christ is Lord, to the glory of God the Father" (Phil. 2:9–11).

"But he, when he had offered one sacrifice for sins for ever, sat down on the right hand of God" (Heb. 10:12); "Who for the joy that was set before him endured the cross, despising shame, and hath sat down at the right hand of the throne of God" (Heb. 12:2). The right hand is the place of honor and power. That is in accord with what Jesus said to his disciples: "All authority hath been given unto me in heaven and on earth" (Matt. 28:18).

What does the exaltation of Christ mean to his people?

1. *An Advocate with the Father*

There is one at the right hand of God to plead our cause: "And if any man sin, we have an Advocate with the Father, Jesus Christ the righteous" (1 John 2:1); "Wherefore also he is able to save to the uttermost them that draw near unto God through him, seeing he ever liveth to make intercession for them" (Heb. 7:25).

The Christian has two intercessors: the Holy Spirit in the heart, and Christ at the right hand of God. Paul tells us about these two intercessors in the eighth chapter of Romans: "The Spirit himself maketh intercession for us with groanings which cannot be uttered" (v. 26); "It is Christ Jesus that died, yea rather, that was raised from the dead, who is at the right hand of God, who also maketh intercession for us" (v. 34).

What can Christ plead as our Advocate? In the earthly courts, the advocate, appearing in behalf of his client, may plead, "Not guilty"; or, "First offense"; or, "Ignorance of the law." But Jesus, our Advocate, can plead none of these things. We are all guilty, and we have sinned many times, and we have knowingly broken God's law. There is but one plea our Advocate can make, his atoning death on the cross.

2. *A Reigning Lord*

In his sermon on the day of Pentecost, Peter said: "Let all the house of Israel therefore know assuredly, that God hath made him both Lord and Christ, this Jesus whom ye crucified" (Acts 2:36).

There are some things to be remembered about the lordship of Christ.

(1) *Absolute lordship.*—It is without limitations or restrictions. It is supreme and authoritative. Where he has spoken, there is an end of all controversy.

He is the head of the church. In its organization, its officers, its ordinances, its mission and message, the church is bound by the lordship of Christ.

The individual Christian knows no master but Christ. Jesus said to his disciples: "Neither be ye called masters: for one is your master, even the Christ" (Matt. 23:10). And again he said: "Ye call me, Teacher, and, Lord: and ye say well; for so I am" (John 13:13).

(2) *Universal lordship.*—It is universal in several respects. It is universal in that it reaches and controls all realms of life. One cannot acknowledge the lordship of Christ in one area of his life, and deny it in another. He is Lord in all areas. He is Lord in one's religious life; he is Lord in one's home life; he is Lord in one's business life; he is Lord in one's social life. He is Lord on Monday, or he is not Lord on Sunday. He is Lord in the home, or he is not Lord in the church. He is Lord in business, or he is not Lord in religion. He is Lord all the time, or he is not Lord at any time. He is Lord everywhere, or he is no Lord anywhere.

His lordship is universal in that it extends to all nations and peoples. There can be no rival to Jesus anywhere on earth. Other religions have their leaders and teachers, but Jesus stands above all. He is not a Lord of mankind, he is the Lord of mankind.

His lordship is universal in that it takes in the whole universe. Paul declared that at the name of Jesus every knee should bow, of things in heaven, and things in earth, and things under the earth. He is Lord on earth, and he is Lord in heaven. He is Lord of men, and he is Lord of angels. He is Lord of the living, and he is Lord of the dead. He is Lord everywhere, and of every creature.

(3) *Final lordship.*—Christ will be Lord to the end of time. He is Lord today, and he will be Lord tomorrow. Sometimes earthly lords are overthrown and replaced by others. Jesus will never be replaced. "Jesus Christ is the same yesterday and to-day, yea and for ever" (Heb. 13:8).

I read of a man who, instead of having figures on the dial of his watch, had the words "Christ is Lord." When asked about it, he said: "It reminds me that Christ is Lord whatever time it is."

3. *A Conquering King*

Isaiah, in describing the coming Messiah, said: "He will not fail nor be discouraged, till he have set justice in the earth; and the isles shall wait for his law" (Isa. 42:4). And in 1 Corinthians 15:25, we read: "For he must reign, till he hath put all his enemies under his feet." There may be seeming defeats along the way, but Jesus will win out in the end.

In the nineteenth chapter of Revelation, John describes a wonderful vision he had. He saw heaven opened, and One riding on a white horse. His eyes were as a flame of fire, and on his head were many crowns. He was clothed in a vesture dipped in blood, and there followed him armies on white horses, and clothed in white. Out of his mouth proceeded a sharp sword. On his vesture and on his thigh a name was written, "KING OF KINGS, AND LORD OF LORDS."

> All hail the power of Jesus' name!
> Let angels prostrate fall;
> Bring forth the royal diadem,
> And crown Him Lord of all.
>
> Ye chosen seed of Israel's race,
> Ye ·ransomed from the fall,
> Hail Him who saves you by His grace,
> And crown Him Lord of all.
>
> Let every kindred, every tribe,
> On this terrestrial ball,
> To Him all majesty ascribe,
> And crown Him Lord of all.
>
> EDWARD PERRONET

6

The Great Salvation

"How shall we escape, if we neglect so great a salvation?"
(Heb. 2:3).

IN THE preceding chapter we discussed God's provision for
the salvation of a lost race, through the gift of his Son. In his
atoning death and glorious resurrection, Christ opened up
the way of salvation for all men. But that does not mean that
all will be saved. There are certain conditions which must
be met before one can be saved.

I. THE EXPERIENCE OF SALVATION

God has but one plan of salvation for all people: "For by
grace have ye been saved through faith; and that not of
yourselves, it is the gift of God" (Eph. 2:8). Salvation is by
the grace of God and is appropriated through personal faith
in the Lord Jesus Christ. God has never had any other plan
of salvation.

Some would have us believe that, during Old Testament
times, men were saved by keeping the law. In his Epistle to
the Galatians and other writings, Paul corrected that false
conception. He declared: "Yet knowing that a man is not
justified by the works of the law but through faith in Jesus
Christ, . . . because by the works of the law shall no flesh
be justified" (Gal. 2:16).

Paul further showed how Abraham and other Old Testament saints were saved through faith, and not by keeping
the law: "Even as Abraham believed God, and it was reck-

oned unto him for righteousness" (Gal. 3:6). Jesus said: "Your father Abraham rejoiced to see my day; and he saw it, and was glad" (John 8:56).

In Hebrews 11:24–26, we find this statement concerning Moses: "By faith Moses, when he was grown up, refused to be called the son of Pharaoh's daughter; choosing rather to share ill treatment with the people of God, than to enjoy the pleasures of sin for a season; accounting the reproach of Christ greater riches than the treasures of Egypt."

These people were saved through faith in Christ who was to come, even as we are saved through faith in the Christ who has come.

There are four important phases in the experience of salvation.

1. *Conversion*

There are two sides to salvation: the divine side, and the human side; God's side, and man's side. The divine side is regeneration, the new birth wrought by the Spirit of God in the heart of the believer. This will be discussed in the following chapter, when we consider the work of the Holy Spirit. More will be said about God's work in salvation further on in this chapter. Here we are dealing with man's part in salvation. We speak of it as conversion. Conversion means a turning. When one experiences conversion, he changes his course. There are two steps in this experience.

(1) *Repentance.*—Before one can be saved, he must repent of his sins. But what is repentance?

First, repentance is more than conviction. One cannot be saved until he feels conviction for his sins. That was the difference between the Pharisee and the publican who went up to the Temple to pray. The Pharisee did not think he was a sinner; he felt no conviction for sin. The publican cried out: "God, be thou merciful to me a sinner" (Luke 18:13). He recognized his sinful condition before God.

But conviction alone is not repentance. One may be deeply convicted of sin, and still not repent. There are few people in the world who have not, at some time, realized that they are sinners. Judas Iscariot realized that he had sinned, but he did not repent. The word which is used concerning him in Matthew 27 : 3, "repented himself," is not the word in the original language which means to repent unto salvation; but is better translated, "felt remorse." He felt sorrow for what he had done, but it was not sorrow that led to repentance, but to suicide.

Second, repentance is more than sorrow for sin. Many people have felt sorrow for their sins who have not repented. The Bible speaks of two kinds of sorrow—godly sorrow and sorrow of the world: "For godly sorrow worketh repentance unto salvation, a repentance which bringeth no regret: but the sorrow of the world worketh death" (2 Cor. 7 : 10).

The sorrow of the world is the kind of sorrow the world feels. It may be sorrow that is caused by the fact that one's sins have been found out, and because he faces the consequences of his sins. That is the reason that so-called death-bed repentance seldom proves to be genuine.

I visited a man some years ago who thought he was going to die. He expressed deep penitence for his sins, but when God let him get well, he went back to the same old manner of life. Godly sorrow is sorrow caused by the realization of the terrible nature of sin. It is something against God. This kind of sorrow is not repentance, but Paul says it leads to repentance.

Third, repentance is a change of mind with respect to sin in its relation to God—hence a change of life. Repentance is turning away from sin in the fear of the Lord. But mere reformation is not true repentance. One may reform for various reasons.

Genuine repentance is an inward experience which manifests itself in an outward change in one's manner of living.

The outward change will be more marked with some than with others. It will depend on how far into sin one has gone. The greater the sins, the more marked will be the outward change.

But repentance is a necessary experience with all, for all have sinned. One is convicted of sin and comes to see sin in its relation to a holy God. He determines in his heart to forsake his sins. The outward change in his manner of life is the fruit of repentance. John the Baptist called on the Pharisees and Sadducees to "bring forth therefore fruit worthy of repentance" (Matt. 3:8), and thus prove that they had really repented.

Fourth, repentance is a necessary experience. Repentance is not salvation, but it is something which accompanies salvation, something without which salvation cannot be experienced. Therefore, the Scriptures are insistent on the necessity for repentance. Jesus said to the people of his day: "Except ye repent, ye shall all in like manner perish" (Luke 13:3).

Fifth, true repentance is accompanied by restitution. When one truly repents, he resolves, not only not to continue in sin, but, insofar as he is able, to make restitution for the sins of the past.

Of course, there are many things one has done for which he cannot make restitution, but there are many things for which he can. If one has been guilty of stealing, repentance means, not only resolving to steal no more, but it means restoring the things he has stolen. When Zacchaeus experienced true repentance, he stood up before the people and said: "If I have wrongfully exacted aught of any man, I restore fourfold" (Luke 19:8).

This, then, is the first step in the experience of conversion, repentance, turning away from all known sin.

(2) *Faith.*—The faith that brings salvation is not faith in a book, though that book be the Bible; not faith in a creed, however orthodox that creed may be; not faith in an institu-

tion, though that institution be a church. The faith that saves is faith in the Lord Jesus Christ.

Paul said he preached: "Repentance toward God, and faith toward our Lord Jesus Christ" (Acts 20:21). Repentance must be toward God, because sin is against God. Faith must be toward the Lord Jesus Christ, for he is the one who has made atonement for our sins.

There are several elements in faith.

First, there is belief. This has been called the intellectual element in faith. In order to be saved, one must believe something. And since faith is toward the Lord Jesus Christ, he must believe something about Christ. He must give intellectual assent to the truth about the person and work of Christ as set forth in the New Testament.

How little one can believe, and still be saved, is not for man to say. I like the statement of a fellow pastor some years ago: "I would rather believe too much than too little." But belief of itself is not saving faith. One may believe all the Bible records concerning Christ, and still not be a Christian.

Second, there must be acceptance. In order to be saved, one must accept Jesus Christ as his own personal Saviour; he must appropriate to himself the saving work of Christ. One may believe that food will sustain life and nourish the body, but he will starve to death unless he partakes of the food. In like manner, one may believe that Jesus Christ died for his sins and made atonement for them, but he will die in his sins unless he accepts Christ as his personal Saviour: "But as many as received him, to them gave he the right to become children of God, even to them that believe on his name" (John 1:12).

Third, faith involves surrender. Saving faith is not only belief in Christ and acceptance of Christ as Saviour, it is surrender to Christ. One is convicted of sin and realizes that he is lost. He sees in Jesus Christ his only hope of salvation and surrenders himself to him.

The experience has been likened to one who has been caught in the rising waters and cut off from land. A rescue boat comes to his aid. The stranded man may believe that the boat will take him safely to shore, and that the boatman is capable of steering it on its course, but he will not be rescued until he climbs into the boat and trusts himself to the boatman's care.

The sinner may believe that Christ has made atonement for his sins, and that he is able to save him from his sins, but he will never be saved until he surrenders himself to Christ.

These are the two steps in conversion: repentance toward God and faith toward the Lord Jesus Christ.

2. *Justification*

The experience of salvation is more than conversion, a turning away from sin, and a turning to the Lord Jesus Christ. It is more than regeneration, a new birth wrought by the Spirit of God. When one repents of his sins and puts his trust in Christ, God forgives his sins. But he does more than that; he restores the sinner to divine favor.

When the prodigal returned home, he asked his father to forgive him and let him have a servant's place in the home. But the father not only forgave him, he restored him to his place in the home and treated him as if he had not gone astray. That is what God does for the sinner who comes to him in penitence and faith. He not only forgives him, but he restores him to divine favor and treats him as if he had not sinned. This is known as justification, the act by which God declares the sinner to be righteous through faith in Christ.

Paul has much to say about justification. He declares that men are justified by faith, and not by the works of the law. One of the most important passages is Romans 5 : 1–2: "Being therefore justified by faith, we have peace with God through our Lord Jesus Christ; through whom also we have had our access by faith into this grace wherein we stand; and we rejoice in hope of the glory of God." These verses declare that justification is an act of God in response to man's faith and results in peace with God, access to divine grace, and abiding joy.

3. *Adoption*

God not only forgives and justifies the believer, he adopts him into his family and makes him his own child: "For ye received not the spirit of bondage again unto fear; but ye received the spirit of adoption, whereby we cry, Abba, Father" (Rom. 8:15).

Wonderful, indeed, it is to be forgiven and restored to divine favor, but it is even more wonderful to be recognized as a child of God. It was wonderful to John, the beloved disciple. As he meditated on this blessed truth, he cried out: "Behold what manner of love the Father hath bestowed upon us, that we should be called children of God; and such we are" (1 John 3:1).

Men are not children of God by nature. They are all "by nature children of wrath" (Eph. 2:3). They become children of God through faith in Christ: "For ye are all sons of God, through faith, in Christ Jesus" (Gal. 3:26).

4. *Sanctification*

It is the nature of normal children to grow. There is something radically wrong if the child remains a child in body or mind. In like manner the child of God is to grow in spiritual stature. When one is born of the Spirit of God, he is just a babe in Christ. But the normal Christian will not remain a babe.

In 1 Peter 2:2, the apostle says: "As newborn babes, long for the spiritual milk which is without guile, that ye may grow thereby unto salvation." And he closes his second epistle with this injunction: "But grow in the grace and knowledge of our Lord and Saviour Jesus Christ."

Paul expressed it in this way: "Till we all attain unto the unity of the faith, and of the knowledge of the Son of God, unto a fullgrown man, unto the measure of the stature of the fulness of Christ: that we may be no longer children, tossed to and fro and carried about with every wind of doctrine" (Eph. 4:13–14).

This growth in Christian experience is known as sanctification. It is not a completed work in this life, as some would claim, but a process that will be completed when the Christian beholds the face of his glorified Lord: "Beloved, now are we children of God, and it is not yet made manifest what we shall be. We know that, if he shall be manifested, we shall be like him; for we shall see him even as he is" (1 John 3:2).

Sanctification starts with an experience—regeneration; it progresses by the operation of the Holy Spirit in the heart and life; it ends in a glorious consummation in the presence of the Lord. The wise man of old said: "The path of the righteous is as the dawning light, that shineth more and more unto the perfect day" (Prov. 4:18). It begins in the dawning light of the new birth, and shines with increasing splendor as the sun rises higher in life's day, and reaches its culmination in the glory of the eternal day.

II. SOME TRUTHS ABOUT SALVATION

Clear thinking and close attention to the Scriptures need to be given to this vital subject, for it is at this point that men most often err.

1. *A Free Gift*

"The free gift of God is eternal life in Christ Jesus our Lord" (Rom. 6:23). Men cannot buy salvation, neither can they earn it by their good works: "For by grace have ye been saved through faith; and that not of yourselves, it is the gift of God; not of works, that no man should glory. For we are his workmanship, created in Christ Jesus for good works, which God afore prepared that we should walk in them" (Eph. 2:8–10).

We are not saved by good works, but for good works. This has been a hard lesson for men to learn. They have insisted on trying to earn salvation by their good deeds or by their good character. But salvation is the free gift of God, and no man can have it until he is willing to accept it as a free gift.

But someone says: "Didn't Paul say, 'Work out your own salvation with fear and trembling' (Phil. 2:12)?" Let us bear in mind that these words were addressed to those who were already Christians. In the next verse Paul says: "For it is God who worketh in you both to will and to work, for his good pleasure." God works it in, man is to work it out.

It is like a father who gives his son a farm. The farm did not cost the son anything, it is a free gift from his father. But what the son makes out of it depends on what he puts into it. If he neglects it, it will grow up in weeds and grass, and produce no harvest. But if he diligently cultivates it, it will bring forth an abundant harvest.

In like manner, salvation is a free gift from God. It does not cost the individual who accepts it anything. But what he makes out of the Christian life depends on what he puts into it. If he is careless and negligent, his life will be one of spiritual poverty. But if he puts his best into it, he will receive an abundant reward. That is what Paul meant when he said: "If any man's work shall abide which he built thereon, he shall receive a reward. If any man's work shall be burned, he shall suffer loss: but he himself shall be saved; yet so as through fire" (1 Cor. 3:14–15).

2. A Personal, Individual Experience

The Word of God magnifies the worth of the individual and the dignity of human personality. In the experience of salvation, God does not deal with people as families or groups. A number of people may be saved at the same time, but each one must experience salvation for himself. "So then each one of us shall give account of himself to God" (Rom. 14:12), is the warning which Paul gave the Roman Christians. This being true, there are two corollary truths that must be emphasized.

(1) *Soul competency.*—The individual is capable of dealing with God for himself. This is sometimes spoken of as soul competency. The individual needs no priest nor sponsor in approaching God. He can come directly to God without the aid of man or institution. He must deal with God for himself, for no one else can answer to God for him. There can be no proxy religion. Parents and friends may help the individual in his approach to God, but they cannot deal with God for him.

(2) *Soul freedom.*—The individual has the right to deal with God for himself, a right which no man can deny him. This is called soul freedom. The individual must be free to read and interpret God's Word for himself, and he must be free to worship God according to the dictates of his own conscience.

Neither man nor institution has any right to stand between a soul and God and hinder that soul in its approach to God. If the individual is to be responsible to God for himself, then he must be free to approach God for himself. Others may help him, but they have no right to hinder him.

3. *A Threefold Experience*

Salvation is in three stages. There is an initial experience—regeneration; a growing experience—sanctification; and a culminating experience—glorification. It is salvation from the guilt of sin, and salvation from the power of sin, and, finally, salvation from the presence of sin. Salvation is in three tenses: past tense, we have been saved—that is regeneration (Eph. 2:5, 8); present tense, we are being saved—that is santification (Phil. 2:12); future tense, we shall be saved—that is glorification (Rom. 5:9; 13:11).

4. *Eternal in Duration*

When one is truly saved, he is saved forever. Jesus said: "My sheep hear my voice, and I know them, and they follow me: and I give unto them eternal life; and they shall never perish, and no one shall snatch them out of my hand. My Father, who hath given them unto me, is greater than all; and no one is able to snatch them out of the Father's hand" (John 10:27-29).

On the human side this is known as the perseverance of the saints. On God's side it is called divine preservation. Saints persevere, and God preserves: "Being confident of this very thing, that he who began a good work in you will perfect it until the day of Jesus Christ" (Phil. 1:6); "Who by the power of God are guarded through faith unto a salvation ready to be revealed in the last time" (1 Peter 1:5).

This is in accord, not only with the promises of God, but with the words which are used to describe salvation. It is a new birth. When one is saved, he is born of God. This is an experience once for all. When one believes on the Lord Jesus Christ, he receives the gift of eternal life: "He that believeth on the Son hath eternal life" (John 3:36). If it is eternal, it cannot cease. It lasts forever.

5. *Calls for Public Confession*

We have these words from Paul: "If thou shalt confess with thy mouth Jesus as Lord, and shalt believe in thy heart that God raised him from the dead, thou shalt be saved: for with the heart man believeth unto righteousness; and with the mouth confession is made unto salvation" (Rom. 10:9-10).

Whether a person who has never made a public confession of his faith in Christ is saved or not, it is not for man to say. But it is certainly true that a person who refuses to make a public confession of his faith can never experience the full satisfactions of his salvation.

6. *Expresses Itself in Obedience*

Here are the words of our Lord: "If a man love me, he will keep my word" (John 14:23); and again: "He that loveth me not keepeth not my words" (v. 24). And the author of Hebrews says: "And having been made perfect, he became unto all them that obey him the author of eternal salvation" (Heb. 5:9). Salvation expresses itself in obedience.

Obedience is both negative and positive. It means abstaining from all evil, keeping oneself unspotted from the world (James 1:27). It also means doing that which is good, dedicating the life to the service of God.

The two sides of obedience are set forth in Romans 12:1-2: "I beseech you therefore, brethren, by the mercies of God, to present your bodies a living sacrifice, holy, acceptable to God, which is your spiritual service. And be not fashioned according to this world: but be ye transformed by the renewing of your mind, that ye may prove what is the good and acceptable and perfect will of God."

7. *Salvation Provided for All People*

The Scriptures declare that God "is longsuffering to youward, not wishing that any should perish, but that all should come to repentance" (2 Peter 3:9); and that he "would have all men to be saved, and come to the knowledge of the truth" (1 Tim. 2:4).

It was God's love for the whole world that led him to send his Son into the world: "For God so loved the world, that he gave his only begotten Son, that whosoever believeth on him should not perish, but have eternal life" (John 3:16).

It was for the salvation of the world that Jesus went to the cross and died: "He is the propitiation for our sins; and not for ours only, but also for the whole world" (1 John 2:2).

God has commissioned his church to give the gospel to the whole world: "Go ye therefore, and make disciples of all the nations" (Matt. 28:19).

It was hard for the Jews to accept this truth. They thought salvation was for the Jews alone. When Peter, under the power of the Holy Spirit, carried the gospel message to the home of Cornelius, it created something of a furor in the church at Jerusalem, which, at that time, was composed of Jewish Christians. But God is no respecter of persons. He has no favorites among the nations. To some he has granted greater opportunities than to others, but greater opportunities always carry with them greater responsibilities.

III. The Doctrine of Election

The Bible doctrine of election has been a stumbling stone to many. The Scriptures declare that God has chosen certain ones for salvation, even before they were born: "For the children being not yet born, neither having done anything good or bad, that the purpose of God according to election might stand, not of works, but of him that calleth, it was said unto her, The elder shall serve the younger. Even as it is written, Jacob I loved, but Esau I hated" (Rom. 9:11–13).

Even stronger is the statement in Ephesians 1:4–5: "Even as he chose us in him before the foundation of the world, that we should be holy and without blemish before him in love: having foreordained us unto adoption as sons through Jesus Christ unto himself, according to the good pleasure of his will."

And in 2 Thessalonians 2:13: "But we are bound to give thanks to God always for you, brethren beloved of the Lord, for that God chose you from the beginning unto salvation in sanctification of the Spirit and belief of the truth." Many other passages in which the doctrine of election is stated might be cited.

Does such a doctrine show partiality on the part of God, and destroy the freedom of the individual? That there is something of mystery in the doctrine, no one will deny. And, certainly, no one would claim to explain it fully. But the Scriptures state that election is based on the foreknowledge of God: "For whom he foreknew, he also foreordained to be conformed to the image of his Son" (Rom. 8:29). "Elect . . . according to the foreknowledge of God the Father, in sanctification of the Spirit, unto obedience and sprinkling of the blood of Jesus Christ" (1 Peter 1:1–2).

God is not limited by time. With him there is no present, past, and future, but one eternal now. He knows all things from the beginning. Thus God's election does not nullify man's freedom of choice. God knows what man's choice will be. These Scripture passages throw some light on the difficult doctrine, but they do not fully explain it.

One does not have to understand all of the doctrines associated with salvation in order to be saved. God has made the plan of salvation so simple and plain that even a child can follow it. He does not say, "Understand, and explain all the truths underlying salvation, and thou shalt be saved," but, "Believe on the Lord Jesus Christ, and thou shalt be saved" (Acts 16:31, KJV).

Many people stumble over the plan of salvation because it is so simple. They feel that they must do something to help God save them. But the Word says, "For by grace are ye saved through faith; and that not of yourselves: it is the gift of God: not of works, lest any man should boast" (Eph. 2:8–9, KJV).

When Christ wanted to explain the plan of salvation, he pointed back to an experience in the wilderness wanderings of the Children of Israel. They had complained because of their hard lot. As a judgment, God sent fiery serpents into their camp, and many of the people were bitten and were dying. Then they cried for mercy. God told Moses to make a brazen serpent, put it on a pole, and lift it up in the midst of the camp. His promise was that if anyone bitten by a serpent would lift his eyes and look upon the brazen serpent, he would be saved from death (see Num. 21:4–9).

Christ made the application. "And as Moses lifted up the serpent...even so must the Son of man be lifted up: that whosoever believeth in him should not perish, but have eternal life" (John 3:14–15, KJV).

7

The Spirit of Power

"But ye shall receive power, when the Holy Spirit is come upon you" (Acts 1:8).

THE FIRST MENTION of the Holy Spirit in the Bible is in the second verse of the first chapter of Genesis: "And the Spirit of God moved upon the face of the waters." Reference is made to the Holy Spirit all through the Old Testament Scriptures, and it is usually in connection with the bestowal of some gift or power.

He endowed men with wisdom and skill: "And I have filled him with the Spirit of God, in wisdom, and in understanding, and in knowledge, and in all manner of workmanship" (Ex. 31:3).

He imparted power for special work: "And, behold, a young lion roared against him. And the Spirit of Jehovah came mightily upon him, and he rent him as he would have rent a kid" (Judg. 14:5-6).

He inspired the prophets to speak God's message: "And the Spirit entered into me when he spake unto me, and set me upon my feet; and I heard him that spake unto me" (Ezek. 2:2).

Peter declared that the Holy Spirit guided the men who wrote the Old Testament Scriptures: "But men spake from God, being moved by the Holy Spirit" (2 Peter 1:21).

But it is in the New Testament that we find the full doctrine of the Holy Spirit.

I. THE PERSON OF THE HOLY SPIRIT

The Holy Spirit is the third person in the Godhead.

93

1. *The Holy Spirit Is a Person*

The word "person" as used in connection with the Trinity is not found in the Scriptures. It is evident that, when so used, it does not mean exactly what it does in our ordinary use of the term. When we speak of a person, we think of an individual separate and distinct from others. But, when speaking of the three persons in the Trinity, we mean what has been described as "inner distinctions in the Godhead."

Dr. Mullins says: "A divine person is not less than a human person, but more." The nature of these distinctions in the Godhead cannot be defined by finite minds.

The Scriptures present the Holy Spirit as a personal being, and not a mere influence or power at work in the world.

(1) *The work he does.*—The Holy Spirit is represented as doing the work of a person. He testifies, he reproves, he comforts, he teaches, he guides, he strives, he helps. Such words as these can be used only of a person.

(2) *The effect of human acts upon him.*—The Holy Spirit is affected as a person by the acts of others. He may be resisted, and grieved, and vexed, and insulted, and blasphemed. Only a person can be so affected by the acts of others.

2. *The Holy Spirit Is God*

The Scriptures represent the Holy Spirit, not only as a person, but as a divine person.

(1) *Called God.*—In his rebuke to Ananias, Peter said: "Why hath Satan filled thy heart to lie to the Holy Spirit?" (Acts 5:3). Then, in the following verse, he said: "Thou hast not lied unto men, but unto God."

(2) *Attributes of God ascribed.*—The Holy Spirit is said to be omnipresent: "Whither shall I go from thy Spirit? Or whither shall I flee from thy presence?" (Psalm 139:7). He is represented as being omniscient: "For the Spirit searcheth all things, yea, the deep things of God" (1 Cor. 2:10).

Omnipotence is ascribed to him: "But all these worketh the one and the same Spirit, dividing to each one severally even as he will" (1 Cor. 12:11).

(3) *Represented as doing the work of God.*—The Holy Spirit convicts of sin; he is the agent in regeneration, or the new birth. In Romans 8:11 the resurrection is said to be the work of the Holy Spirit: "But if the Spirit of him that raised up Jesus from the dead dwelleth in you, he that raised up Christ Jesus from the dead shall give life also to your mortal bodies through his Spirit that dwelleth in you."

II. THE PROMISE OF THE HOLY SPIRIT

While there were manifestations of the Holy Spirit all through the Old Testament dispensation, there was to be a special manifestation of his presence and power. He was to come in a definite manner and abide in the world.

1. *Old Testament Prophecies*

Many centuries before Pentecost the coming of the Holy Spirit was foretold: "And it shall come to pass afterward, that I will pour out my Spirit upon all flesh; and your sons and your daughters shall prophesy, your old men shall dream dreams, your young men shall see visions: and also upon the servants and upon the handmaids in those days will I pour out my Spirit" (Joel 2:28–29). On the great day of Pentecost, Peter quoted that promise and declared that it was fulfilled in the events of that day (Acts 2:17–18).

2. *The Promise of Jesus*

It was Jesus who gave definite promises concerning the coming of the Holy Spirit. In his parting message to his disciples in the upper room, he said: "And I will pray the Father, and he shall give you another Comforter, that he may be with you for ever, even the Spirit of truth" (John 14:16–17). "But the Comforter, even the Holy Spirit, whom the Father will send in my name, he shall teach you all things" (John 14:26). "For if I go not away, the Comforter will not come unto you; but if I go, I will send him unto you" (John 16:7). On the day of his ascension, he said to his disciples: "And behold, I send forth the promise of my Father upon you: but tarry ye in the city, until ye be clothed with power from on high" (Luke 24:49).

III. THE COMING OF THE HOLY SPIRIT

We have a record of this great event in Acts 2:1–4: "And when the day of Pentecost was now come, they were all together in one place. And suddenly there came from heaven a sound as of the rushing of a mighty wind, and it filled all the house where they were sitting. And there appeared unto them tongues parting asunder, like as of fire; and it sat upon each one of them. And they were all filled with the Holy Spirit, and began to speak with other tongues, as the Spirit gave them utterance."

Several facts concerning the coming of the Holy Spirit are worthy of special note.

1. *A Definite Event*

The coming of the Holy Spirit was just as definite as the birth of Jesus. There will never be another Pentecost any more than there will be another incarnation of the Son of God. There may be pentecostal experiences, when men and women yield their lives more fully to the Holy Spirit, but there will never be another Pentecost like that of the upper room. Those who point to Pentecost as authority for the so-called second blessing have missed the mark. Pentecost was the definite coming of the Holy Spirit to take up his work in the world.

2. *Once for All Time*

In his promise of the coming of the Holy Spirit, Jesus said: "And I will pray the Father, and he shall give you another Comforter, that he may be with you for ever" (John 14:16). The Holy Spirit has been in the world for nearly two thousand years, and he will abide here until the end of time.

3. *Accompanied by Signs*

Note the suggestive symbols:

(1) *The sound as of the rushing of a mighty wind (Acts 2:2).*—The record does not say the wind was the Holy Spirit; but the coming of the Holy Spirit was accompanied by a sound as of a rushing mighty wind, which was a symbol of the Holy Spirit. Our Lord described the Holy Spirit in the same way: "The wind bloweth where it will, and thou hearest the voice thereof, but knowest not whence it cometh, and whither it goeth: so is every one that is born of the Spirit" (John 3:8).

This symbolism of the Holy Spirit suggests power. There is tremendous power in the rushing of a mighty wind, a power that uproots trees and demolishes strong buildings. The Holy Spirit is the Spirit of power.

(2) *Tongues like fire.*—Again, the record does not say the Holy Spirit was fire; but his coming was accompanied by the appearance of tongues, parting asunder, like as of fire.

Fire is both a cleansing and destructive agent. Metals are put into the fire to burn out the dross. The one is consumed, and the other is purified. In like manner, the Holy Spirit cleanses the life from evil. When he comes in, sin must go out.

4. *Produced Transforming Results*

The result of the Holy Spirit's coming may be summed up in one word—power. That is what Jesus said his coming would mean: "But ye shall receive power, when the Holy Spirit is come upon you" (Acts 1:8). And he told his disciples to wait until that power came: "But tarry ye in the city, until ye be clothed with power from on high" (Luke 24:49). The coming of the Holy Spirit was marked by wonderful power. It was not physical power, but spiritual power.

(1) *Transforming power.*—The coming of the Holy Spirit changed that band of men and women in the upper room from a frightened group, behind closed doors, into a courageous band that threw open the locked doors, and went out into the crowded streets of the city to proclaim the gospel of a crucified and risen Lord.

(2) *Enlightening power.*—Gathered in Jerusalem at that time were people from all over the Roman Empire, speaking different languages. The Holy Spirit bestowed upon the disciples the power to speak these various tongues: "And they were all filled with the Holy Spirit, and began to speak with other tongues, as the Spirit gave them utterance" (Acts 2:4).

(3) *Convicting power.*—Under the preaching of Peter, the multitude was convicted of sin: "Now when they heard this, they were pricked in their heart, and said unto Peter and the rest of the apostles, Brethren, what shall we do?" (Acts 2:37).

(4) *Saving power.*—When Peter told them what to do, they obeyed. "They then that received his word were baptized: and there were added unto them in that day about three thousand souls" (Acts 2:41).

IV. The Work of the Holy Spirit

Jesus told of many things the Holy Spirit would do. His work falls under three heads.

1. *In the Individual*

What does the Holy Spirit do in, and for, the individual?

(1) *Conviction.*—The Holy Spirit convicts the individual of sin. He reveals to him something of the nature of sin and the consequences of sin, and awakens in him a realization of his own guilt before a holy God.

The Spirit uses various means in bringing conviction. Sometimes it is the public proclamation of the gospel, as on the day of Pentecost. Sometimes it is the testimony of another, as in the case of David (2 Sam. 12:13). Sometimes it is a terrifying experience, as in the case of the Philippian jailer.

(2) *Regeneration.*—When one is convicted of sin, he may do one of two things: he may harden his heart and resist the Holy Spirit, or he may open his heart by faith and let the Holy Spirit come in. When he follows the latter course, the Holy Spirit enters his heart and performs a work of grace so transforming that it is called regeneration, or a new birth.

The old man of sin is put to death, and a new man in Christ is born. One may not be able to understand how this change is wrought, but he can experience it. The blind man whose eyes Jesus opened said there was much about it that he did not understand, but of one thing he was sure: "Whereas I was blind, now I see" (John 9:25).

Our Lord declared that the experience of regeneration is necessary before one can get into the kingdom of God: "Verily, verily, I say unto thee, Except one be born of water and the Spirit, he cannot enter into the kingdom of God" (John 3:5).

(3) *Sanctification.*—"Sanctify" means to make holy. Sanctification is the process of making holy. Sanctification is the work of the Holy Spirit: "Being sanctified by the Holy Spirit" (Rom. 15:16).

Conviction is the work of the Holy Spirit when he comes to the door of the heart and knocks; regeneration is the work of the Holy Spirit when he enters into the heart after the door has been opened by faith; sanctification is the work of the Holy Spirit as he abides in the heart.

Sanctification is growth in the Christian life, and, like physical growth, it is a gradual process. It begins with regeneration and ends with glorification. Some people grow faster than others, and some people grow taller than others; but, in every normal life, there is spiritual growth and development. This growth will be in proportion to the fulness of the Spirit in the heart and life.

(4) *Consolation.*—The Holy Spirit is the great Comforter of human hearts. When Jesus told his disciples that he was going away, their hearts were filled with sorrow: "Because I have spoken these things unto you, sorrow hath filled your heart" (John 16:6). But he assured them that the Comforter would come and bring them peace and joy: "And I will pray the Father, and he shall give you another Comforter, that he may be with you for ever, even the Spirit of truth" (John 14:16–17). That is part of the work of the Holy Spirit, to bring comfort to sorrowing hearts.

(5) *Illumination.*—The Holy Spirit reveals truth to the mind and heart of the believer. He is the great Teacher. Jesus said: "Howbeit when he, the Spirit of truth, is come, he shall guide you into all the truth" (John 16:13).

The Spirit enlightens the minds of believers so that they may understand the truth of God's Word: "Now the natural man receiveth not the things of the Spirit of God: for they are foolishness unto him; and he cannot know them, because they are spiritually judged" (1 Cor. 2:14). The Bible, in its deepest meaning, is a closed book to those who have not the Spirit of God.

(6) *Intercession.*—As has been stated before, the Christian has two intercessors: Christ at the right hand of the Father, and the Holy Spirit in the heart. In Romans 8:26–27, the intercessory work of the Holy Spirit is stated: "And in like manner the Spirit also helpeth our infirmity: for we know not how to pray as we ought; but the Spirit himself maketh intercession for us with groanings which cannot be

uttered; and he that searcheth the hearts knoweth what is the mind of the Spirit, because he maketh intercession for the saints according to the will of God." With these two intercessors, one in heaven and the other on earth, the Christian is well fortified.

The work of the Holy Spirit in the lives of believers is summed up in the name which was given him—Paraclete. This is a transliteration of the Greek word *Parakletos,* which means called to one's side, hence, a helper. The Holy Spirit is the Christian's Helper in every needed way.

This designation of the Holy Spirit as "Paraclete" is confined to the writings of John. In the Authorized Version, it is translated by the English word "Comforter." There is no one English word which conveys the full meaning of the Greek word. The Holy Spirit is all that the different words indicate, and more. He is Teacher, Guide, Comforter, Intercessor, etc. He meets every need of the Christian.

2. *In the Church*

The Scriptures tell us that the Holy Spirit dwells in the church. The church is called the temple of the Holy Spirit. To the church at Corinth, Paul wrote: "Know ye not that ye are a temple of God, and that the Spirit of God dwelleth in you?" (1 Cor. 3:16). And to the Ephesians he wrote: "In whom ye also are builded together for a habitation of God in the Spirit" (Eph. 2:22).

What is the Spirit's work in the church? Several things may be mentioned briefly.

(1) *Edification.*—"So the church throughout all Judaea and Galilee and Samaria had peace, being edified; and, walking in the fear of the Lord and in the comfort of the Holy Spirit, was multiplied" (Acts 9:31). The Holy Spirit builds up the church.

(2) *Guidance.*—"And as they ministered to the Lord, and fasted, the Holy Spirit said, Separate me Barnabas and Saul

for the work whereunto I have called them" (Acts 13:2).
"For it seemed good to the Holy Spirit, and to us, to lay upon
you no greater burden than these necessary things" (Acts
15:28). Thus the Holy Spirit led the church at Antioch to
launch the great missionary enterprise, and guided the church
at Jerusalem in settling a difficult question.

(3) *Bestowal of gifts.*—Listen to Paul's words to the
church at Corinth: "Now there are diversities of gifts, but the
same Spirit. . . . But to each one is given the manifestation of
the Spirit to profit withal. For to one is given through the
Spirit the word of wisdom; and to another the word of knowledge, according to the same Spirit: to another faith, in the
same Spirit; and to another gifts of healings, in the one Spirit;
and to another workings of miracles; and to another prophecy; and to another discernings of spirits: to another divers
kinds of tongues; and to another the interpretation of
tongues: but all these worketh the one and the same Spirit,
dividing to each one severally even as he will" (1 Cor. 12:4–
11).

(4) *Empowering for service.*—"But ye shall receive power,
when the Holy Spirit is come upon you" (Acts 1:8). That was
the promise of the risen Lord to his disciples. It was in the
power of the Holy Spirit that the early church went forth to
win victories. Without the Holy Spirit, the church is a weak
and helpless organization.

3. *In the World*

Concerning the work of the Holy Spirit, Jesus said: "And
he, when he is come, will convict the world in respect of sin,
and of righteousness, and of judgment: of sin, because they
believe not on me; of righteousness, because I go to the Father, and ye behold me no more; of judgment, because the
prince of this world hath been judged" (John 16:8–11).

By "the world," Jesus meant the evil, unbelieving world.

It is the same word which James used when he said: "Ye adulteresses, know ye not that the friendship of the world is enmity with God? Whosoever therefore would be a friend of the world maketh himself an enemy of God" (James 4:4). And it is the word John used when he said: "Love not the world, neither the things that are in the world. If any man love the world, the love of the Father is not in him" (1 John 2:15).

The word "convict" is also translated convince, or reprove. It carries the idea of convincing by presenting proof. The Holy Spirit convicts the world of three things.

(1) *Conviction of sin.*—"Of sin, because they believe not on me." The Holy Spirit convicts the world of the reality of sin, and the nature of sin. He shows that the one great sin of all is the sin of unbelief. Jesus didn't say: "Of sin, because they are adulterers, or murderers, or drunkards," but, "because they believe not on me." That was the sin of which the world of that day was guilty, and it is the sin of which the world of this day is guilty.

(2) *Conviction of righteousness.*—"Of righteousness, because I go to the Father, and ye behold me no more." The Jewish leaders accused Jesus of being a sinner: "We know that this man is a sinner" (John 9:24). Jesus claimed to be righteous: "Which of you convicteth me of sin?" (John 8:46). His resurrection and return to the Father was proof of his righteousness.

No man can claim righteousness for himself, for all have sinned. Through his atoning death, his resurrection, and return to the Father, Christ offers imputed righteousness to those who believe: "But now apart from the law a righteousness of God hath been manifested, being witnessed by the law and the prophets; even the righteousness of God through faith in Jesus Christ unto all them that believe" (Rom. 3:21–22); "And be found in him, not having a righteousness

of mine own, even that which is of the law, but that which
is through faith in Christ, the righteousness which is from
God by faith" (Phil. 3:9).

(3) *Conviction of judgment.*—"Of judgment, because the
prince of this world hath been judged." Sin brings judgment.
This is proved by the judgment that fell on Satan, the prince
of this world. At the cross he thought he had gained his
greatest victory. But it turned out to be his greatest defeat.
There he was judged and condemned.

If the Prince of this world has been condemned, then
those who are of the world will surely be judged. When Paul
stood before Felix, "he reasoned of righteousness, and self-
control, and the judgment to come" (Acts 24:25).

V. THE FRUIT OF THE HOLY SPIRIT

If the Holy Spirit abides in the life, his presence will be
manifested by certain virtues and graces which only the
Holy Spirit can produce. Paul calls these the fruit of the
Spirit: "But the fruit of the Spirit is love, joy, peace, longsuffering, kindness, goodness, faithfulness, meekness, self-
control" (Gal. 5:22–23). It is like a vine with three clusters
of fruit.

1. *Fruit in the Inner Life*

The first cluster is that which manifests itself in the inner
life—love, joy, peace. The love spoken of here is not the sen-
timent which is often called love. It is something deeper, and
broader, and higher, and grander than that. It is a fundamental, governing principle of the life, something which only
the Spirit of God can produce.

Along with love goes joy. There is a vast difference between joy and pleasure. Pleasure is dependent on outward
conditions, but joy wells up within the heart, and is inde-

pendent of outward conditions. The world can give pleasure, but it cannot give joy.

Then comes peace. When the Holy Spirit abides in the heart, he gives peace—peace to the conscience that has known the hurt of sin, peace to the heart that has been broken, peace to the soul that has been troubled.

2. Fruit in the Outward Life

The second cluster is the fruit which manifests itself in the outward life—longsuffering, kindness, goodness. Longsuffering means calm endurance in the face of injustice. It is the capacity to receive ill-treatment without striking back, to deal with irritating people without becoming irritated, to keep one's temper in the face of abuse and slander.

Then comes kindness. This is a step beyond patience. Patience is passive; it is remaining still. Kindness is active; it is doing something to help others. Kindness wins when cruelty fails.

Following kindness is goodness. This is a twofold grace. It means purity of life, and it means unselfish service. Goodness is more than kindness. Kindness is helping when the opportunity is presented, but goodness seeks the opportunity. Goodness is righteousness at work.

3. Fruit in One's Relation to Himself

The third cluster is the fruit manifested in one's relations to himself—faithfulness, meekness, self-control. Faithfulness means fidelity, loyalty—loyalty to men and loyalty to God.

Meekness does not mean weakness. Jesus was meek, but he was no weakling. Meekness is the opposite of a proud, boastful, unforgiving spirit.

Following meekness is self-control. What a time men have controlling themselves! They have wrestled with the appetites, and passions, and evil tendencies of their own natures, and have gone down in defeat. The only power on earth that can make a man master himself is the Spirit of God.

VI. MAN'S RESPONSE TO THE HOLY SPIRIT

The New Testament mentions several attitudes which people may take in their response to the Holy Spirit.

1. *One May Resist the Holy Spirit*

This is the word which Stephen used in addressing those who opposed his ministry: "Ye stiffnecked and uncircumcised in heart and ears, ye do always resist the Holy Spirit: as your fathers did, so do ye" (Acts 7:51). That is the attitude of the unbeliever who hardens his heart against the Holy Spirit. And the Christian is sometimes guilty of resisting the Spirit, when he refuses to obey the impulses which the Spirit plants in his heart.

2. *One May Insult the Holy Spirit*

That is the word which Moffatt uses in translating Hebrews 10:29: "Who has insulted the Spirit of grace." The word is used of those upon whom the Holy Spirit has moved mightily. It is closely akin to the unpardonable sin. They who are guilty of insulting the Holy Spirit are those who have wantonly and arrogantly rejected him, and driven him from their lives.

3. *One May Grieve the Holy Spirit*

Paul was writing to Christians when he used this word: "And grieve not the Holy Spirit of God, in whom ye were sealed unto the day of redemption" (Eph. 4:30). Of course, the Holy Spirit is grieved by unbelievers when they resist him, but he is also grieved by Christians when they neglect and disobey him. It is the picture of a father grieving over a rebellious and wayward son.

4. *One May Quench the Holy Spirit*

Paul was addressing the Christians at Thessalonica when he used this word: "Quench not the Spirit" (1 Thess. 5:19). The figure is that of putting out a fire by pouring water upon it. The Holy Spirit is described as being like fire. His coming on the day of Pentecost was accompanied by tongues like fire. He kindles the fires of love and zeal in the heart of the Christian. One may quench the Spirit by indifference, and neglect, and disobedience.

5. *One May Be Filled with the Holy Spirit*

This is the ideal toward which Paul exhorted the Ephesian Christians: "And be not drunken with wine, wherein is riot, but be filled with the Spirit" (Eph. 5:18). There is a difference between having the Holy Spirit and being filled with the Holy Spirit.

Every Christian has the Holy Spirit: "But if any man hath not the Spirit of Christ, he is none of his" (Rom. 8:9). It is the coming of the Holy Spirit into the heart with his regenerating power that makes one a Christian. However, one may have the Holy Spirit without being filled with the Holy Spirit. One may be a Christian without being a Spirit-filled Christian.

A Christian is likened unto a vessel. Christ said of Saul of Tarsus: "For he is a chosen vessel unto me" (Acts 9:15). And Ananias said to Saul: "The Lord, even Jesus, who appeared unto thee in the way which thou camest, hath sent me, that thou mayest receive thy sight, and be filled with the Holy Spirit" (Act 9:17).

Two conditions must be met before a vessel can be filled.

(1) *Emptied.*—A vessel cannot be filled with clean water until it is emptied of unclean water. And before a Christian can be filled with the Spirit, he must be emptied—emptied of self, emptied of sin, emptied of everything that is out of

harmony with the Spirit of God. A person cannot hold on to anything that is unclean and be filled with the Holy Spirit.

(2) *Surrendered.*—Before a vessel can be filled, it must be given up for the use of the one who would fill it. And a Christian cannot be filled with the Spirit until he yields himself fully to the Spirit.

Let us change the figure. A person has a house to let. But he has some things which he wishes to keep in the house. So he puts these things in one room, locks the door, and puts the key in his pocket. He says to the renter: "You may have the use of all the house except this one room. I have reserved that for myself."

That is the way some people treat the Holy Spirit. There is something in their lives that they are not willing to give up; there is a room which they are not willing to surrender. So they lock the door to that room and say to the Holy Spirit: "You may have all of my life except that one room. I have reserved that for myself." That person cannot be filled with the Spirit.

Dr. A. J. Gordon used to tell about an American and an English friend who were viewing the Niagara Rapids. The American said to his English friend, "Come, and I'll show you the greatest unused power in the world." Then, taking him to the foot of Niagara Falls, he said, "There is the greatest unused power in the world." "Not so, my friend," was the reply. "The greatest unused power in the world is the Holy Spirit of the Living God."

There is no substitute for this power, either in the individual life, or in the church. We are inclined to boast of our numbers, our organizations, and our gifts. We thank God for these, but it will be a sad day for the church if it magnifies these things to the neglect of the Holy Spirit. It is true today, as it was in the day of Zerubbabel: "Not by might, nor by power, but by my Spirit, saith Jehovah of hosts" (Zech. 4:6).

Suppose the group in the upper room, after praying for a week, had said, "Our Lord has given us a great work to do. We have no time to lose. Let us go out and start to work." What a failure they would have made! But when the Holy Spirit came and filled them, they went forth with transforming powers and witnessed the salvation of three thousand souls in a single day.

8

The Church Established by Christ

"Upon this rock I will build my church" (Matt. 16:18).

THE LORD made provision whereby his work would be carried on after his departure. He established the church (Matt. 16:18) and sent his Holy Spirit to empower it (John 15:26). That means that the church is a divine institution, divinely conceived, divinely planned, and divinely commissioned.

The word "church" is used in the New Testament with a twofold meaning. It usually refers to a local congregation, but in some instances it does refer to the whole body of believers. In this chapter we are discussing the church as a local congregation, though the two uses of the word cannot always be clearly dissociated.

I. THE NATURE OF THE CHURCH

What is a church? In the New Testament the word is never used to designate a building. Neither does it mean a national or worldwide organization. In the local sense it may be briefly defined as a company of baptized believers, voluntarily associated in covenant relations, organized according to the New Testament pattern, and living in obedience to Christ, the great head of the church.

In this brief definition some characteristics of a true church are set forth. It is a *company*. The Greek word for church means called out. Originally this word referred to the assembly of people who were called out of their homes and places of business to give consideration to matters of public interest.

Our Lord used the word "church" to designate the company of his disciples. They were called-out people. But not every company of people is a church. The church is a company of *believers*.

None but believers have membership in the church. But not every company of believers constitutes a church. It must be a company of *baptized* believers.

There is no record in the New Testament of any but baptized believers in the church. But not every company of baptized believers can be called a church. It must be a company *organized according to the New Testament pattern.* But it takes still more to make a true church.

A church is a company of baptized believers, voluntarily associated in covenant relations, according to the New Testament pattern, and *pledged to live in obedience to Christ, the great head of the church.* A true church is an active body, a working organization.

Two statements may be made concerning the nature of the church.

1. *A Living Organism*

One of the most suggestive figures used of the church is that of a body, of which Christ is the head: "And he put all things in subjection under his feet, and gave him to be head over all things to the church, which is his body" (Eph. 1:22–23). "And he is the head of the body, the church" (Col. 1:18). "For even as we have many members in one body, and all the members have not the same office: so we, who are many, are one body in Christ, and severally members one of another" (Rom. 12:4–5).

The figure of the church as the body of Christ is described more fully in 1 Corinthians 12:12–27. As the body is made up of many members, varying in size and function, but all working together, so the church is composed of many members, differing in age and ability, but all working together under the leadership of Christ.

This means that a church is more than an organization; it is an organism, a living thing. As the body of Christ, it is the agency through which Christ does his work in the world.

2. *A Spiritual Temple*

To the church at Corinth, Paul wrote: "Know ye not that ye are a temple of God, and that the Spirit of God dwelleth in you?" (1 Cor. 3:16). In the Old Testament we have the material Temple, the Temple built of wood and stone. In the New Testament we have the spiritual temple, built of living stones, redeemed men and women: "Ye also, as living stones, are built up a spiritual house" (1 Peter 2:5).

The material Temple was built for a dwelling place of God. Concerning the Temple which he built, Solomon said: "Jehovah hath said that he would dwell in the thick darkness. But I have built thee a house of habitation, and a place for thee to dwell in for ever" (2 Chron. 6:1–2).

God promised that he would dwell in that Temple: "And the word of Jehovah came to Solomon, saying, Concerning this house which thou art building, if thou wilt walk in my statutes, and execute mine ordinances, and keep all my commandments to walk in them; then will I establish my word with thee, which I spake unto David thy father. And I will dwell among the children of Israel, and will not forsake my people Israel" (1 Kings 6:11–13).

As the dwelling place of God, the temple must be kept holy. On two occasions Jesus cleansed the Temple in Jerusalem. Surely, he is equally zealous to keep his spiritual temple holy: "If any man destroyeth the temple of God, him shall God destroy; for the temple of God is holy, and such are ye" (1 Cor. 3:17).

In the Old Testament Temple there were certain men set

apart as priests, to minister before the Lord. This was a privilege that belonged to only a few. But in the New Testament church, all are priests unto God: "But ye are an elect race, a royal priesthood, a holy nation" (1 Peter 2:9); "And he made us to be a kingdom, to be priests unto his God and Father" (Rev. 1:6).

One of the duties of the priests was to offer sacrifices. So Peter says: "Ye also, as living stones, are built up a spiritual house, to be a holy priesthood, to offer up spiritual sacrifices, acceptable to God through Jesus Christ" (1 Peter 2:5). The sacrifices offered up in the spiritual temple are spiritual sacrifices. What are they?

(1) *The sacrifice of a broken and contrite heart.*—David realized this: "For thou delightest not in sacrifice; else would I give it: thou hast no pleasure in burnt-offering. The sacrifices of God are a broken spirit: a broken and a contrite heart, O God, thou wilt not despise" (Psalm 51:16–17). No other sacrifice can be acceptable to God until there is the sacrifice of a broken and contrite heart.

(2) *The sacrifice of praise.*—In Hebrews 13:15, we have this injunction: "Through him then let us offer up a sacrifice of praise to God continually, that is, the fruit of lips which make confession to his name."

(3) *The sacrifice of good deeds.*—Again, in Hebrews 13:16, we read: "But to do good and to communicate forget not: for with such sacrifices God is well pleased."

(4) *The sacrifice of a dedicated life.*—One of the most familiar verses in the Bible is Romans 12:1: "I beseech you therefore, brethren, by the mercies of God, to present your bodies a living sacrifice, holy, acceptable to God, which is your spiritual service."

II. The Organization of the Church

What is the New Testament pattern for the organization of the church? There are two main characteristics.

1. *A Democracy*

Several things are involved in this.

(1) *Voluntary membership.*—The church is made up of people who voluntarily enter its fellowship. No one is a member of the church by birth. And no one is to be brought into the church against his will. Each one is to make his own choice. Others may seek to influence him and may help him in making his choice, but the decision rests with him.

(2) *Equality of privileges.*—In the church each member has equal rights and privileges with all others. The old and the young, the rich and the poor, the educated and the ignorant—all stand on equal footing. Some, by reason of natural ability and training, will become leaders; but they have no right to lord it over their brethren.

(3) *Self-government.*—The church is a self-governing body. There is no individual or organization above the church which has any authority over it. Every church, under God, manages its own affairs, without let or hindrance from others. And there is no governing body within the church. Governmental authority rests with the members, but this should always be in accordance with divine authority. All matters of polity or policy are settled by a vote of the congregation in dependence upon the Holy Spirit's guidance.

2. *An Independent Organization*

A church should co-operate with others, but its affairs are never to be controlled by others.

(1) *In its relation to other churches.*—No church, however strong and influential, has any authority over another church, no matter how small that church may be. No group of churches can tell another church what it must, or must not, do. They may offer advice, but the individual church will decide what it will do.

(2) *In its relation to denominational bodies.*—There are

associations and conventions in which messengers from the churches meet for counsel and co-operation, but these bodies can exercise no authority over individual churches.

Co-operation, and no coercion, is the principle by which churches are guided, and by which they are bound together in fellowship and service. Of course, there must be agreement in doctrine and practice, for "shall two walk together, except they have agreed?" (Amos 3:3).

(3) *In its relation to civil government.*—The state is to exercise no control over any church or religious organization. No church or any religious organization is to exercise any authority over the state. They belong to different spheres and must be kept separate and distinct, insofar as any union is concerned.

But church and state each have certain claims which must be respected. Jesus said: "Render therefore unto Caesar the things that are Caesar's; and unto God the things that are God's" (Matt. 22:21). Church members should be good citizens of the state, obeying the laws of the state, so long as those laws do not violate the law of God. And the state must give protection to the churches and their work, so long as the church does not infringe on the rights of the state.

III. THE OFFICERS OF THE CHURCH

The two church officers mentioned in the New Testament are pastor and deacon. In 1 Corinthians 12:28, Paul says: "And God hath set some in the church, first apostles, secondly prophets, thirdly teachers, then miracles, then gifts of healings, helps, governments, divers kinds of tongues." However, these seem to refer to men who were endowed with special gifts for special service, and not to church officers.

1. *The Pastor*

This is the name commonly used today, but it is found but

once in the New Testament: "And he gave some to be apostles; and some, prophets; and some, evangelists; and some, pastors and teachers" (Eph. 4:11). In the New Testament this officer is called "elder," or "bishop," which means overseer. Thus we have three names for the same officer: pastor, elder, and bishop.

It has been suggested that perhaps our Baptist forefathers abandoned the use of the name "bishop," or "elder" because of the unscriptural associations which came to be connected with these names, and made use of the name which had no such unscriptural associations—"pastor," which means shepherd.

In the New Testament churches there seems to have been more than one pastor in a church. Just how many, we are not told. The number was probably determined by the size of the church. In addressing his epistles to the churches, Paul always used the plural number in referring to this officer: "To all the saints in Christ Jesus that are at Philippi, with the bishops and deacons" (Phil. 1:1). When he landed at Miletus, "he sent to Ephesus, and called to him the elders of the church" (Acts 20:17).

(1) *The qualifications of the pastor.*—These are set forth in 1 Timothy 3:1–7, and in Titus 1:6–9. They include upright character, an untarnished reputation, qualities of leadership, and ability to teach. In short, the pastor must be endowed by nature, by grace, and by training. It is a high standard, and no one who does not strive to reach that standard has any place in the ministry.

(2) *The duties of the pastor.*—These are implied in the names given to this officer. He is called "elder," which means older. This name suggests experience, and one worthy of respect. The name "bishop" means overseer. He is to keep watch over the church, leading and directing it in its work. "Pastor" means shepherd. The shepherd leads his flock, feeds his flock, and protects his flock. He seeks the wandering sheep

and ministers to the weak and helpless. So the pastor is to be preacher, teacher, leader, and counselor.

(3) *The support of the pastor.*—Paul emphasizes the fact that pastors are to receive adequate support from those to whom they minister. To the church at Corinth, he said: "Know ye not that they that minister about sacred things eat of the things of the temple, and they that wait upon the altar have their portion with the altar? Even so did the Lord ordain that they that proclaim the gospel shall live of the gospel" (1 Cor. 9:13–14).

When our Lord sent forth his disciples to preach and minister to the people, he told them to take no money with them, "for the laborer is worthy of his hire" (Luke 10:7). The pastor is to be "no lover of money" (1 Tim. 3:3), but he is to receive adequate support from those to whom he ministers.

2. The Deacon

The name "deacon" means minister, or servant. Originally it was used of anyone who served, whether in the home, or in the state, or in the church. But, in the course of time, it came to be used of those who were selected for special duties in the church. The pastors and the deacons are usually mentioned together in the New Testament: "To all the saints in Christ Jesus . . . at Philippi, with the bishops and deacons" (Phil. 1:1). Paul puts them together in giving their qualifications in the third chapter of 1 Timothy.

(1) *Origin of the office.*—The story of the origin of the office of deacon is found in the sixth chapter of Acts, though the name does not occur. They were seven in number, but this does not mean that every church is to have just seven deacons. The number will depend on the size of the church. Three or four may be enough for some churches, while fifty may not be too many for other churches. These first deacons were chosen by the whole congregation and were set apart by the apostles for their service by the laying on of hands and prayer.

(2) *Qualifications of the deacon.*—We find these qualifications stated in Acts 6:3 and in 1 Timothy 3:8–13. The qualifications of a deacon are very similar to those of a bishop. Good character and an untarnished reputation are essential in a deacon. Of course, there are other qualifications, such as business ability and qualities of leadership; but no matter what other qualifications one may have, if he is lacking in character, he is not fit to be a deacon.

(3) *Duties of the deacon.*—These are not clearly defined in the New Testament. The first deacons were chosen to look after the administration of the common fund, in order that the apostles might have more time for prayer and the ministry of the word. But they were also to be spiritual leaders in the church. This is indicated by the high standard of character that was demanded.

The deacon is to be the pastor's helper in all the activities of the church. Certainly, his duties consist in more than passing the plates for the offering and ministering at the Lord's table.

IV. The Ordinances of the Church

There were two rites in the New Testament churches which were later called "ordinances." These ordinances have no saving efficacy and possess no power of themselves to impart a blessing. They are symbols of important truths and are to be observed in obedience to the command of our Lord.

1. *Baptism*

This ordinance has been the subject of much controversy through the years, largely because many people have gotten their conception of it from the writings of men rather than from the New Testament. What saith the Scriptures?

(1) *The origin.*—The ordinance of baptism was first used by John the Baptist, who was divinely commissioned: "There

came a man, sent from God, whose name was John" (John
1:6). God sent him, not only to preach repentance unto the
remission of sins, but to baptize those who repented as an
outward symbol of the inward change: "But he that sent me
to baptize in water" (John 1:33).

Jesus gave his sanction to the ordinance by submitting to
baptism, as recorded in Matthew 3:13–17, and by his parting
command to his disciples: "Go ye therefore, and make disciples of all the nations, baptizing them into the name of the
Father and of the Son and of the Holy Spirit" (Matt. 28:19).
So baptism is a voluntary act on the part of the individual, in
obedience to the command of his Lord.

(2) *The act.*—Baptism is immersion in water. That is the
meaning of the Greek word from which we get the word
"baptism." And it is the only act that fits into the descriptions
of baptism which we have in the New Testament: "And they
both went down into the water, both Philip and the eunuch;
and he baptized him. And when they came up out of the
water, the Spirit of the Lord caught away Philip" (Acts 8:38–
39). That language pictures immersion.

Paul describes baptism as a burial and resurrection: "We
were buried therefore with him through baptism into death:
that like as Christ was raised from the dead through the glory
of the Father, so we also might walk in newness of life. For
if we have become united with him in the likeness of his
death, we shall be also in the likeness of his resurrection"
(Rom. 6:4–5).

(3) *The subjects.*—Believers are the only proper subjects
of baptism. This is set forth both by the examples and by the
teaching of the New Testament. There is no record in the
New Testament of the baptism of any who were not believers
or who did not profess to be believers.

The necessity of faith in Christ as a prerequisite to true
baptism is illustrated in the story of the men at Ephesus, as

recorded in Acts 19:1–5. These men had submitted to John's baptism evidently without saving faith in Christ. When they were led to exercise true faith in the Saviour, they were baptized into the name of the Lord Jesus. The first act was not true baptism, because it was not believer's baptism.

(4) *The symbolism.*—Three truths are symbolized in the ordinance of baptism. It points back to the burial and resurrection of our Lord. It proclaims a transforming experience in the believer's life, the death of the old man of sin, and the raising up of a new man in Christ. It expresses the blessed hope of a glorious resurrection of the body at the return of the Lord.

2. *The Lord's Supper*

This ordinance has also been the subject of much controversy, both as to its meaning, and its observance.

(1) *A memorial rite.*—The Lord's Supper was instituted by our Lord in the upper room just before his death on the cross. It was to be observed as a memorial of his atoning death. When he gave the broken bread to his disciples, he said: "Take, eat; this is my body" (Matt. 26:26). And when he gave them the cup, he said: "Drink ye all of it; for this is my blood of the covenant, which is poured out for many unto remission of sins" (Matt. 26:27–28).

There is no spiritual efficacy in the bread and wine themselves; they are memorials of the broken body and shed blood of the Saviour. The one great purpose in the observance of the ordinance is to proclaim the death of our Lord: "For as often as ye eat this bread, and drink the cup, ye proclaim the Lord's death till he come" (1 Cor. 11:26).

(2) *A church ordinance.*—The Lord's Supper is a church ordinance, to be observed by the church, and participated in by those who have met the conditions laid down in the New Testament—saving faith, baptism, and church membership.

3. *The Heart of the Gospel*

The two ordinances symbolize the two truths which stand at the heart of the gospel, the atoning death, and the glorious resurrection of our Lord. To the Corinthian Christians, Paul wrote: "Now I make known unto you, brethren, the gospel which I preached unto you, which also ye received, wherein also ye stand, by which also ye are saved, if ye hold fast the word which I preached unto you, except ye believed in vain. For I delivered unto you first of all that which also I received: that Christ died for our sins according to the scriptures; and that he was buried; and that he hath been raised on the third day according to the scriptures" (1 Cor. 15: 1–4). For the sake of the truths which they symbolize, the ordinances must be kept true to the New Testament pattern.

V. THE WORK OF THE CHURCH

Christ established the church as the agency through which to carry on his work in the world. The church is to worship, proclaim, educate, and minister to all the needs of mankind, but its chief business is to worship God. The work of the church, then, is both local and worldwide. Jesus outlined the work of the church when he said: "And ye shall be my witnesses both in Jerusalem, and in all Judaea and Samaria, and unto the uttermost part of the earth" (Acts 1:8). They were to begin at home, but they were not to stop there. On another occasion Jesus said: "The field is the world" (Matt. 13:38).

1. *In the Community*

The church carries on its work in the community by maintaining public worship and ministering to the needs of the people, both physical and spiritual. But the emphasis must ever be on the spiritual.

The church seeks to bring the lost to a saving knowledge of Christ through the public proclamation of the gospel, and by personal witness. It reaches out a helping hand to those who are in need, both in the church and out of the church. It strives to maintain a high standard of morality and to establish righteousness and justice in all the relations of life.

The church can do its best work only as it maintains a high standard of life among its own members. It can never win the world by compromising with the world. For its own sake, and for the sake of the work, the church must maintain a healthy discipline. Every effort should be made by a church to help its members live up to the standards set by Jesus Christ.

2. *In the World*

In carrying out its world mission, the individual church co-operates with other churches in sending the gospel to all nations, and in ministering to their needs. This is the meaning of associations and conventions.

Through such co-operation that churches can best promote the Master's program. The churches furnish the workers for the various fields and provide the means by which the work is to be carried on. This calls for stewardship of prayer, of life, and of material possessions.

9

The World to Come

"And tasted the good word of God, and the powers of the age to come" (Heb. 6:5).

ON TWO OCCASIONS Jesus spoke of "the world to come," or "the age to come" (Matt. 12:32; Mark 10:30). The same expression occurs twice in the book of Hebrews (2:5; 6:5). The contrast is between the present world, or age, and the coming age. Some people become so absorbed in the things of this world that they forget there is a world to come.

Our knowledge of the world to come is limited. There are many things about it that we do not know. But enough has been revealed to give us all we need to know.

I. DEATH

Physical death is the common lot of all: "And inasmuch as it is appointed unto men once to die" (Heb. 9:27). All who have lived on earth have died, with two glorious exceptions, Enoch and Elijah: "By faith Enoch was translated that he should not see death" (Heb. 11:5). "And it came to pass, as they still went on, and talked, that, behold, there appeared a chariot of fire, and horses of fire, which parted them both asunder; and Elijah went up by a whirlwind into heaven" (2 Kings 2:11). All who are now living on earth will die, unless the Lord should come in this generation.

What is death? That is as hard a question to answer as, What is life? Death is not cessation of being. It marks the end of life on earth, but, when one dies, he does not cease to exist. Jesus said; "And be not afraid of them that kill the body, but are not able to kill the soul" (Matt. 10:28).

Death is the separation of soul and body. The wise man stated it in this way: "And the dust returneth to the earth as it was, and the spirit returneth unto God who gave it" (Eccl. 12:7). Sometimes death is described as "giving up the spirit." That is the expression used concerning the death of Jesus—Jesus, when he had cried again with a loud voice, "yielded up his spirit" (Matt. 27:50).

There are two figures of speech used in the New Testament to describe death. The first one refers to the body, and is called a sleep. At death the body seems to fall asleep. We find this expression "asleep" used several times. The story of the death of Stephen closes with these words: "And when he had said this, he fell asleep" (Acts 7:60). And of David it was said, "After he had in his own generation served the counsel of God, fell asleep" (Acts 13:36).

Paul comforted the Thessalonian Christians concerning their dead by saying, "But we would not have you ignorant, brethren, concerning them that fall asleep; that ye sorrow not, even as the rest, who have no hope" (1 Thess. 4:13). The word "sleep" would suggest also the idea of an awakening. At death the body falls asleep, but there will be an awakening at the resurrection.

The second figure used concerning death has reference to the soul, or spirit, and is spoken of as a departure. That was a favorite figure of Paul: "Having the desire to depart and be with Christ" (Phil. 1:23). In speaking of his own death, which he realized was not far off, he said: "The time of my departure is come" (2 Tim. 4:6). It is the picture of a ship, weighing anchor and putting out to sea.

So, at death, the body is laid to rest in the bosom of the earth; but the spirit takes its departure into another world where it will live forever.

II. The Intermediate State

This refers to the place and condition of the dead between death and the resurrection. Where does one go when he dies? Whither does the spirit take its departure? There is a Hebrew word in the Old Testament—*sheol*—whose equivalent in the New Testament is the Greek word *Hades*. Unfortunately, in the King James Version, these words are translated hell. But this is a mistranslation, which has been corrected in the later versions. The word means the abode of the dead, without any reference to the condition of the dead. All who have died are in Hades.

This does not mean that hell has been abolished. There is a word which is correctly translated hell—*Gehenna*—and it was this word that our Saviour used, when he said: "It is good for thee to enter into life maimed, rather than having thy two hands to go into hell, into the unquenchable fire" (Mark 9:43).

Certain truths about the state of the dead are revealed in the Scriptures.

1. *The Righteous*

What becomes of the soul of the Christian when he dies? Some say it sleeps in the grave with the body. Such a view is in plain contradiction of certain passages of Scripture. Jesus said to the thief on the cross, "To-day shalt thou be with me in Paradise" (Luke 23:43). In speaking of his own death, Paul said, "Having the desire to depart and be with Christ" (Phil. 1:23). In Revelation 14:13 we have this blessed assurance: "Blessed are the dead who die in the Lord from henceforth."

Three truths are thus revealed concerning the righteous dead: they are in paradise; they are with Christ; and they are happy. This contradicts any doctrine of a purgatory,

where the souls of the righteous must go through a period
of suffering before they can be made ready for entrance into
the blessedness of the redeemed.

2. *The Wicked*

The Scriptures reveal very little about the condition of the
wicked between death and the resurrection. There are two
passages that give us about all the knowledge we have on
this subject. In the parable of the rich man and Lazarus,
Jesus said: "The rich man also died, and was buried. And in
Hades he lifted up his eyes, being in torments" (Luke
16:22–23). In 2 Peter 2:9 we have this description of the
unrighteous dead: "The Lord knoweth how to deliver the
godly out of temptation, and to keep the unrighteous under
punishment unto the day of judgment." Just as the righteous
dead are in the presence of the Lord in a state of blessedness,
so the wicked dead are separated from the Lord and are in
a state of misery.

III. THE RETURN OF CHRIST

Because there have been so many theories concerning the
second coming of Christ, some have ceased to stress the
doctrine. It is set forth in the Word of God as the blessed hope
of Christians: "Looking for the blessed hope and appearing
of the glory of the great God and our Saviour Jesus Christ"
(Titus 2:13).

Here, again, we are limited in our knowledge. It is always
dangerous to go beyond that which has been revealed in the
Scriptures. But there are several truths which are made
known concerning the return of Christ.

1. *The Certainty of His Return*

There is no truth more plainly stated in the Word of God
than this. Only a few passages can be given here.

When the disciples stood on the Mount of Olives, gazing up into the heavens after their departing Lord, "two men stood by them in white apparel; who also said, Ye men of Galilee, why stand ye looking into heaven? this Jesus, who was received up from you into heaven, shall so come in like manner as ye beheld him going into heaven" (Acts 1:10–11).

Paul said, "For the Lord himself shall descend from heaven, with a shout, with the voice of the archangel, and with the trump of God" (1 Thess. 4:16). And in Hebrews 9:28: "Christ . . . shall appear a second time, apart from sin, to them that wait for him, unto salvation."

Jesus said to his disciples: "Ye heard how I said to you, I go away, and I come unto you" (John 14:28). He had much to say to his disciples about being ready for his return. The twenty-fourth chapter of Matthew, and kindred passages in the other Gospels, deal at length with the Lord's return. To make the coming of death the fulfilment of these promises is to do violence to the Scriptures.

2. The Nature of His Return

Several things are revealed about this.

(1) *Personal and visible.*—The two men who appeared to the disciples on the Mount of Olives said: "This Jesus, who was received up from you into heaven, shall so come in like manner as ye beheld him going into heaven" (Acts 1:11). He will come back in the same personal way in which he departed. And his coming will be visible to all: "Behold, he cometh with the clouds; and every eye shall see him" (Rev. 1:7). His return, then, will be more than a spiritual coming.

(2) *Sudden and unexpected.*—That is the description which Jesus himself gave of his return. It will be with the suddenness of the lightning flash: "For as the lightning cometh forth from the east, and is seen even unto the west; so shall be the coming of the Son of man" (Matt. 24:27). The

peoples of the world will not be expecting it: "For as in those days which were before the flood they were eating and drinking, marrying and giving in marriage, until the day that Noah entered into the ark, and they knew not until the flood came, and took them all away; so shall be the coming of the Son of man" (Matt. 24:38–39).

(3) *With great glory.*—"When the Son of man shall come in his glory, and all the angels with him" (Matt. 25:31); "Then shall they see the Son of man coming in clouds with great power and glory" (Mark 13:26). "For whosoever shall be ashamed of me and of my words, of him shall the Son of man be ashamed, when he cometh in his own glory, and the glory of the Father, and of the holy angels" (Luke 9:26).

3. *The Time of His Coming*

Much of the confusion concerning the second coming of Christ has arisen from the efforts on the part of men to set a time for his return. There has not been a time since his departure that there were not some people who were expecting him to return in their generation. It is well for us to keep in mind the things our Lord said about his return.

(1) *Time known only by the Father.*—We have these words of Jesus in Mark 13:32: "But of that day or that hour knoweth no one, not even the angels in heaven, neither the Son, but the Father."

This is one of the secrets the Father has locked up in his own heart. And it is best that it should be so. Suppose men knew when the Lord would return. If the glorious event were near at hand, there would be confusion such as existed in Thessalonica in the days of Paul.

If the time were known to be in the distant future, men would disregard it entirely. But, because no man knows when it will be, all should live in readiness. "Therefore be ye also ready; for in an hour that ye think not the Son of man cometh" (Matt. 24:44).

(2) *Warning against prying into God's secrets.*—It is not for men to pry into the secrets which God has not seen fit to reveal. When the disciples inquired of their risen Lord concerning the time of the restoration of the kingdom to Israel, he replied, "It is not for you to know times or seasons, which the Father hath set within his own authority" (Acts 1:7).

(3) *An attitude of expectancy.*—The attitude on the part of God's people is to be one of expectancy. The Lord may return at any time. Jesus said, "Watch therefore: for ye know not on what day your Lord cometh" (Matt. 24:42). The best preparation for the Lord's return is to be busy in the work he has given us to do. "Blessed is that servant, whom his lord when he cometh shall find so doing" (Matt. 24:46).

4. *The Millennium*

A discussion of the time of our Lord's return raises the much debated question concerning the millennium. The word comes from a Latin word, which means a thousand years. This period of a thousand years is mentioned only once in the Bible, Revelation 20:1–10. There are difficulties encountered in interpreting this passage in a book of the Bible which contains so many figures and symbols. However, there are other passages of Scripture which throw light on the subject.

There are two schools of interpreters, which have been designated as premillennialists and postmillennialists. Only a brief outline of the teachings of these two schools can be given here.

(1) *Premillennialists.*—According to this school, the world will grow more and more wicked, culminating in the return of Christ. There will be two aspects of his coming.

First, there will be a coming for his saints. At this time, the dead in Christ shall be raised, and living Christians will be changed, and together they will be caught up in the clouds to meet the Lord. This is sometimes called the Rapture and is described in 1 Thessalonians 4:15–17. There will follow a period of tribulation on the earth, during which time Israel will be converted and become messengers of the gospel.

Second, there will be a coming with his saints. At the close of the tribulation period, Christ will return with his saints, and the judgment of the nations will follow. Satan will be bound, and Christ will reign with his saints for a thousand years. At the end of that period, Satan will be loosed, and the great battle of Armageddon will occur, in which Christ will win his final victory, and Satan will be cast into the lake of fire. Then will follow the resurrection of the wicked and the judgment before the great white throne.

(2) *Postmillennialists.*—According to this school of interpreters, there will be a gradual triumph of the gospel in the world, culminating in a period of righteousness, justice, and peace, which will continue for a thousand years. Some modern interpreters make the millennium an indefinite period of time, extending from the crucifixion to the end of time. At the appearance of Christ, there will be a general resurrection of the dead, both righteous and wicked, followed by the judgment.

Probably a majority of Christian people today feel that it is more important to be busy in the work of the Lord than to debate about the exact interpretations and details relative to our Lord's return. Some of these people call themselves *amillennialists.* Assuredly, the certain fact of Christ's coming and his triumph on which all agree, should be our constant hope and inspiration.

IV. The Resurrection

While good Christian people may differ in their views concerning two resurrections, one of the righteous and one of the wicked, all agree that both the righteous and wicked will be raised from the dead. This is clearly taught in both the Old and New Testament Scriptures. In Daniel 12:2, we find this statement of the truth: "And many of them that sleep in the dust of the earth shall awake, some to everlasting life, and some to shame and everlasting contempt." And Paul says: "Having hope toward God, which these also themselves look for, that there shall be a resurrection both of the just and unjust" (Acts 24:15).

The same questions which men were asking about the resurrection in the days of Paul are still being raised: "But some one will say, How are the dead raised? and with what manner of body do they come?" (1 Cor. 15:35). The fact of the resurrection of the body should not be hard for those who believe in God to accept. As Paul said to Agrippa, "Why is it judged incredible with you, if God doth raise the dead?" (Acts 26:8).

If God made the body of man out of the dust in the beginning, can he not raise up the body out of the dust? Redemption will not be complete until the resurrection. When a Christian dies, his spirit goes to be with the Lord, but his body is buried in the ground. Is that to be the end of it? "Not so," say the Scriptures. It will be raised again, a redeemed body, fitted for the redeemed spirit.

What will be the nature of the risen body? Little is revealed in the Scriptures about the resurrection of the wicked, but there are many truths about the resurrection of the righteous. The resurrection of Christ gives us the assurance and pattern of the resurrection of his people. Two facts are made clear.

1. *Identity Preserved*

The resurrection body will, in a real sense, be identical with the mortal body. The body of Jesus came out of the tomb. He showed himself alive to his disciples and revealed to them the marks of the nails in his hands. It was, in some real sense, the same body that had been laid in the tomb. So it will be with the resurrection bodies of God's people.

2. *Changed Bodies*

The resurrection body will be different from the mortal body. Paul says: "Flesh and blood cannot inherit the kingdom of God; neither doth corruption inherit incorruption" (1 Cor. 15:50). He describes the change that takes place after this manner: "It is sown in corruption; it is raised in incorruption: it is sown in dishonor; it is raised in glory: it is sown in weakness; it is raised in power: it is sown a natural body; it is raised a spiritual body" (vv. 42–44).

From the foregoing we learn that the resurrection body will be incorruptible, powerful, glorious, and spiritual. It will be like the body of the glorified Christ: "For our citizenship is in heaven; whence also we wait for a Saviour, the Lord Jesus Christ: who shall fashion anew the body of our humiliation, that it may be conformed to the body of his glory" (Phil. 3:20–21). "It is not yet made manifest what we shall be. We know that, if he shall be manifested, we shall be like him; for we shall see him even as he is" (1 John 3:2).

V. The Judgment

Some interpreters believe there will be more than one judgment, while others think there will be but one. However, all agree on the fact of the judgment. The New Testament contains such definite statements as these: "Inasmuch as he hath appointed a day in which he will judge the world in righteousness" (Acts 17:31); "And inasmuch as it is appointed unto men once to die, and after this cometh judgment" (Heb. 9:27).

1. *The Purpose*

The purpose of the judgment is not to determine destiny. This is forever fixed when one dies. There will be no second chance in the world to come. Dr. A. H. Strong says: "The object of the final judgment is not the ascertainment, but the manifestation, of character, and the assignment of outward condition corresponding to it." [2]

Paul says, "For we must all be made manifest before the judgment-seat of Christ; that each one may receive the things done in the body, according to what he hath done, whether it be good or bad" (2 Cor. 5:10).

The purpose of the judgment will be the bestowal of rewards and penalties. Not all who are saved will receive the same reward, and not all who are lost will receive the same degree of condemnation. God will render unto everyone according to his works. Both rewards and penalties will be according to opportunity and conduct.

2. *The Person*

The Scriptures declare that Christ will be the judge: "Inasmuch as he hath appointed a day in which he will judge the world in righteousness by the man whom he hath ordained; whereof he hath given assurance unto all men, in that he hath raised him from the dead" (Acts 17:31). "For we must all be made manifest before the judgment-seat of Christ" (2 Cor. 5:10).

The One who presents himself as Saviour is the One before whom men must stand to be judged. One day Jesus stood before Pilate: one day Pilate must stand before Jesus.

3. *The Nature*

Just what is to be the nature of this final judgment?

(1) *Personal.*—"So then each one of us shall give account

---

[2] *Systematic Theology,* p. 582

of himself to God" (Rom. 14:12). The individual will not be lost in the multitude. And each one will give account of himself, and not of another.

(2) *Universal.*—It will include all people. "For we shall all stand before the judgment-seat of God" (Rom. 14:10). No one will escape. "And I saw the dead, the great and the small, standing before the throne" (Rev. 20:12).

(3) *Thorough.*—It will include thoughts, words, and deeds. "Wherefore judge nothing before the time, until the Lord come, who will both bring to light the hidden things of darkness, and make manifest the counsels of the hearts" (1 Cor. 4:5). Jesus said: "And I say unto you, that every idle word that men shall speak, they shall give account thereof in the day of judgment" (Matt. 12:36). And, in Revelation 20:13, we read: "And they were judged every man according to their works."

(4) *Just and impartial.*—God is no respecter of persons. A man's standing on earth will have nothing to do with his standing before God. And there will be no mistakes, no miscarrying of justice. Everyone will receive his just deserts.

(5) *Final.*—There will be no appeal from that judgment; there will be no second trial. The judgment of that day will stand forever.

VI. The Final State

Following the judgment, both the righteous and wicked enter into their final state, which is eternal in duration.

1. *The Righteous*

The final state of the righteous may be viewed from two standpoints.

(1) *Their condition.*—The Scriptures speak of the righteous as entering into eternal life: "And these shall go away into eternal punishment: but the righteous into eternal life"

(Matt. 25:46). Every Christian is possessor of eternal life: "He that believeth on the Son hath eternal life" (John 3:36). But the glorious consummation is in the world to come.

Eternal life is infinitely more than eternal existence. It refers, not so much to the quantity, but to the quality of life. It is the life of God in the soul. It is life in all of its fulness, and glory, and power; life without the limitations of earth. Jesus said: "And this is life eternal, that they should know thee the only true God, and him whom thou didst send, even Jesus Christ" (John 17:3). It is a life of fellowship with God, and of joyous service.

(2) *Their abode.*—The final abode of the righteous is known as heaven. Jesus described it as a real place: "I go to prepare a place for you. And if I go and prepare a place for you, I come again, and will receive you unto myself; that where I am, there ye may be also" (John 14:2-3).

Heaven is described in the Word of God under various figures, but no figure of speech can adequately portray its glory. Everything that causes pain and sorrow are shut out: "And death shall be no more; neither shall there be mourning, nor crying, nor pain, any more" (Rev. 21:4). Heaven will include everything that will satisfy the deepest longings of the soul—rest, and peace, and joy, and fellowship, and service.

2. *The Wicked*

The final state of the wicked may also be considered from two standpoints.

(1) *Their condition.*—As the righteous enter into eternal life, so the wicked enter into eternal death. But just as eternal life does not refer, primarily, to eternal existence, so eternal death does not mean cessation of being. It is separation from God and the glory of life eternal. Just as the condition of the righteous is one of peace and joy, so the condition of the wicked is that of misery and suffering: "There shall be the

weeping and the gnashing of teeth, when ye shall see Abraham, and Isaac, and Jacob, and all the prophets, in the kingdom of God, and yourselves cast forth without" (Luke 13:28).

(2) *Their abode.*—The final abode of the wicked is called hell. This, too, is a real place. It is described in figurative language, but that does not do away with its terrible reality. Jesus spoke of it as outer darkness and as a place "where their worm dieth not, and the fire is not quenched" (Mark 9:48). The abode of the wicked is real and eternal.

As we think of these things, John 3:16 becomes more precious: "For God so loved the world, that he gave his only begotten Son, that whosoever believeth on him should not perish, but have eternal life." And we are made to feel more of our responsibility for sharing the gospel of salvation with a world that is lost in sin.

SUGGESTIONS FOR THE TEACHER

Who Will Lead in the Study of This Book

I. GENERAL SUGGESTIONS

You will need to be certain in your own mind about what you believe in respect to each of the doctrines discussed in this book. You will also need to be able to state your belief clearly and to justify it from the Scriptures. Consult as many of the doctrinal books in Subject Area 33 as you can, reading particularly the discussions of those doctrines on which you need further information.

CONSIDERING THE LEARNERS

You will be safe in assuming that your class members need much help in understanding basic Baptist doctrines and their implications or derivatives. They also need help in expressing their beliefs clearly. They may or may not be aware of their needs.

Perhaps some members can tell of personal experiences in which they have been embarrassed because they could not make clear—perhaps to a person of another faith—the position of Baptists on a certain point, and the reason for our stand. Others may express confusion because Baptists do not all think alike on many facets of doctrine. Read 1 Peter 3:15 as a motto.

STATING THE TEACHING PURPOSE

Lead the class as a group to confront the question: Why do we need to study a book on Baptist doctrine? List the various responses, and then ask the class members to propose an aim or learning goal for the course. The statement should be simple but clear-cut, somewhat as follows: *To clarify our understanding of what we believe and why.* The group may wish to add: *To begin to see the relationship between our doctrines and our methods of work.*

PROCEDURES

Effective teaching of this book will almost certainly involve lecture, as the class follows an outline, but other procedures should also be used.

Role playing.—For an example of this technique, designate one class member to take the part of a college student who will confront a friend with the question: What makes you think that the Bible is inspired—any more than Tennyson or Shakespeare or Milton was inspired? Another class member takes the part of a Christian friend who answers the student.

A similar technique may be used for presenting other questions.

Bible using.—Adults learn skills in Bible using by facing situations in which they need such skills.

Seek to give practice in the use of a concordance. Key words may be used at the appropriate points in this study particularly if the class shows need for practice in using a concordance.

Plan for use of the center column helps in a reference Bible (or footnotes in versions other than AV). For example, in connection with Chapter 3, read Psalm 8 : 4–8. Use the center references to find other verses that deal with the dignity and destiny of man.

Activities or projects.—Study is enriched by group activities which continue throughout the course.

Suggest to the class that they constitute themselves a committee of the whole to draw up a confession of faith, such as might be prepared for adoption by a new church when it is constituted. After a basic doctrine has been discussed in class, the group would seek to reduce the discussion to a one paragraph statement of belief relative to that doctrine. This activity would be repeated as a summary of the study for each chapter in the book.

Each class member may prepare a dictionary of doctrinal terms. Every chapter introduces some words with a specific doctrinal or theological meaning. List these words as they occur. Let the group discuss the meaning and agree on a definition, which each member will record. At the close of the study course, the list of words may be alphabetized and kept for future reference. (If the church has facilities for reproducing material—mimeograph, ditto, etc.— the class may elect a secretary to record each definition as it is agreed upon, and then to alphabetize the list and have copies made for each member.)

Seeing applications.—Constantly confront the class members with questions to bring out the practical significance of the doctrines studied. For example:

Do our beliefs in regard to the Bible and the competency of each individual to approach God make it obligatory for a Baptist to engage in personal Bible study?

How do our beliefs about man relate to our efforts at reaching more people through our Sunday schools and other church organizations? State the doctrinal explanation of why we (1) baptize only believers; (2) require a person to be baptized before he becomes a member of the church; (3) do not have a governed body to tell each church how to conduct its affairs; (4) seek to have every church member participate in financial support of the church?

Personal evaluations.—From time to time ask: Have you had any problems cleared up by this discussion? Have you gained new knowledge? Of what practical significance will the understanding of this particular doctrine be to you?

VISUAL AIDS

Contact your nearest Baptist Film Center for related films and filmstrips.

II. TEACHING SUGGESTIONS

Chapter 1

To prompt class discussion, ask the following questions. What do you mean when you say the Bible is inspired? What difference does one's concept of inspiration make in one's use of the Bible (1) as a source of doctrine and (2) as a guide for personal daily living? What is the distinctive Baptist doctrine in regard to the authority of the Scriptures?

Chapter 2

Using a reasonably complete concordance, find five or more verses which make some significant claim about "the name of the Lord."

Chapter 3

Further study may involve research into the doctrines of creation, man, the fall, sin, and Satan. Books in Subject Area 33 of the New Church Study Course will be helpful for this additional study.

Chapter 4

The author lists five tactics that Satan "used in the beginning and has continued to use" in tempting mankind to sin. Referring to the five methods named, ask members of the group to share examples of how similar tactics are used in tempting people today.

For an outside project, ask some of the group members to make a comparison of the author's discussion of sin with the discussion found in other books on Baptist doctrine, particularly the books in Section 33 of the New Church Study Course. In class share and discuss the reports made by the group members.

Ask class members to prepare a list of verses they would use to show an unsaved person that he is a sinner and needs a Saviour.

Chapter 5

Lead the group in a search of the Scriptures dealing with the preexistence of Christ. Using a Bible with center column references, locate the Scripture passages the author uses to show the preexistence of Christ. From the references which are cited in the center column find other passages which teach that Christ existed before his conception and birth in Bethlehem.

Two errors in concept about Christ have been abroad even from the early days of Christianity. One claims that he was merely man—the best man who ever lived. The other claims that he was God, but not really a man. For a project assignment, either within the class or between sessions, ask the group members to find Scripture passages in addition to those cited by the author.

For class discussion, ask why the resurrection is fundamental to all Christian belief.

Chapter 6

This chapter uses many great doctrinal words or phrases, each of which represents a basic Baptist doctrine: salvation, conversion, repentance, faith, justification, adoption, sanctification, soul competency, soul freedom, perseverance of the saints, preservation of the saints (eternal security), confession, election. Let an individual or committees each volunteer to take one of these terms and look up the discussion of the doctrine in as many books as possible from Subject Area 33, then formulate a statement of the doctrine involved. Share these statements in class discussion.

Chapter 7

Give emphasis to the five ways an individual may respond to the Holy Spirit. Ask the class to give illustrations of each of the responses—either from their own life or the lives of others.

Chapter 8

As a class activity, draw up a statement that summarizes all the work of a New Testament church.

Chapter 9

After discussion of the subject material in this chapter, ask group members to share any previous misconceptions which now have been clarified. Then ask the group members to present questions on related subjects which have not been clarified.

PERSONAL LEARNING ACTIVITIES

Chapter 1

1. The Bible is inspired in the sense that it was written by _____ who were inbreathed by the _____ _____.
2. The Bible is a book of rules. (True or False)
3. The Bible is authoritative in the realm of _____ (choose one: science, religion, history, business, all of these.)

Chapter 2

4. Four biblical statements descriptive of God are _____, _____, love, and _____ _____ _____.
5. In describing God as "infinite," we mean he is without _____ or _____.
6. God as Father has a _____ and _____ relationship with us.
7. The doctrine of the Trinity teaches that we have three Gods. (True or False)

Chapter 3

8. "Adam" is a proper name. (True or False)
9. Man is made in the image of God in terms of personality, _____, and _____.
10. In the book of Revelation, Satan is called "the _____ of the whole world."
11. The Bible reveals Satan to be the chief of _____ (choose one: the world, mankind, evil spirits, sinners).
12. One result of the fall was the _____ of man's nature.

Chapter 4

13. The root meaning of the word "sin" is "to _____" the mark.
14. The nature of sin could be classified _____ (choose one: deception, rebellion, transgression, all of these.)
15. One word which best describes the consequences of sin is _____.

Chapter 5

16. The Bible tells us nothing about Christ before his birth. (True or False)
17. The word which describes God becoming man is _____.

18. The _____ of Christ sets Christianity apart from all other religions.

Chapter 6

19. The two steps in the salvation experience are _____ and _____.

20. Faith involves _____, acceptance, and _____.

21. "The act by which God declares the sinner to be righteous through faith in Christ" is a definition of the word _____. (Choose one: justification, sanctification, adoption.)

Chapter 7

22. The power given by the Holy Spirit can be described by the words _____, enlightening, _____, and _____.

23. The Holy Spirit works with the _____, the church, and the _____.

Chapter 8

24. The church is a _____ institution.

25. The church is more than an organization, it is an _____.

26. According to the New Testament, a larger church may give advice to a smaller church. (True or False)

27. The church ordinances are _____ and _____.

Chapter 9

28. Two figures of speech describing death are _____ and _____.

29. *Hades* is another word for hell. (True or False)

30. The time of Jesus' return is known only by _____.

THE CHURCH STUDY COURSE

The Church Study Course is a Southern Baptist education system consisting of short courses for adults and youth combined with a credit and recognition system. Also available in the system are noncredit short courses (called foundational units) for children and preschoolers. The courses in the Church Study Course are for use in addition to the ongoing study and training curricula made available to churches by the denomination.

More than five hundred courses are available in twenty-three subject areas. Courses are flexible enough to offer credit for either individual or group study. Credit is awarded for each course completed. These credits may be applied to one or more of the one hundred plus diploma plans in the system. Diplomas are available for most leadership positions as well as general diplomas for all Christians. These diplomas are the certification that a person has completed from five to eight prescribed courses. Diploma requirements are given in the catalogs.

Enrollment in a diploma plan is made by completing Form 725, Church Study Course Enrollment/Credit Request, and sending it to the Awards Office at the Sunday School Board. Course credit may also be requested on this form. A permanent record of courses and diplomas will be maintained by the Awards Office. Twice each year up-to-date reports called "transcripts" will be sent to churches to distribute to members participating in the Church Study Course. Each transcript will list courses and diplomas completed and will show progress toward diplomas currently being sought. The transcript will show which courses are needed to complete diploma requirements. A diploma will be issued automatically when the final requirement is met.

Complete details about the Church Study Course system, courses available, and diplomas offered may be found in a current copy of *Church Study Course Catalog* and in the study course section of *Church Materials Catalog*. Study course materials are available from Baptist Book Stores.

The Church Study Course system is simple enough to be administered by volunteer workers with limited time. The system is universal so that credit earned in one church is recognized in all other Southern Baptist churches. More than 600,000 awards are earned by adults and youth each year.

The Church Study Course is promoted by the Sunday School Board, 127 Ninth Avenue, North, Nashville, Tennessee 37234; by Woman's Missionary Union, P.O. Box C-10, Birmingham, Alabama 35283-0010; by the Brotherhood Commission, 1548 Poplar Avenue, Memphis, Tennessee 38104; and by the respective departments of the state conventions affiliated with the Southern Baptist Convention.

How to Request Credit for This Course

This book is the text for a course number 05003 in subject area: Baptist Doctrine. The course is designed for five hours of group study.

Credit for this course may be obtained in two ways:

1. Read the book and attend class sessions. (If you are absent from one or more sessions, complete the Personal Learning Activities for the material missed.)
2. Read the book and complete the Personal Learning Activities. (Written work should be submitted to an appropriate church leader.)

A request for credit may be made on Form 725, Church Study Course Enrollment/Credit Request, and sent to the Awards Office, Sunday School Board, 127 Ninth Avenue, North, Nashville, Tennessee 37234. The form on the following page may be used to request credit.

A record of your awards will be maintained by the Awards Office. Twice each year copies will be sent to churches for distribution to members.

CHURCH STUDY COURSE
ENROLLMENT/CREDIT REQUEST (FORM-725)

PERSONAL CSC NUMBER (If Known)

INSTRUCTIONS:
1. Please PRINT or TYPE.
2. COURSE CREDIT REQUEST—Requirements must be met. Use exact title.
3. ENROLLMENT IN DIPLOMA PLANS—Enter selected diploma title to enroll.
4. For additional information see the Church Study Course Catalog.
5. Duplicate additional forms as needed. Free forms are available from the Awards Office and State Conventions.

TYPE OF REQUEST: (Check all that apply)
- ☐ Course Credit
- ☐ Enrollment in Diploma Plan
- ☐ Address Change
- ☐ Name Change
- ☐ Church Change

REQUEST FOR

☐ Mr.   ☐ Miss
☐ Mrs.

DATE OF BIRTH → Month | Day | Year

Name (First, MI, Last)

Street, Route, or P.O. Box

City, State, Zip Code

CHURCH

Church Name

Mailing Address

City, State, Zip Code

COURSE CREDIT REQUEST

Course No		Title
05003	Use exact title 1.	*These Things We Believe*
Course No.	Use exact title 2.	
Course No	Use exact title 3.	
Course No.	Use exact title 4.	
Course No.	Use exact title 5.	

ENROLLMENT IN DIPLOMA PLANS

If you have not previously indicated a diploma(s) you wish to earn, or you are beginning work on a new one(s), select and enter the diploma title from the current Church Study Course Catalog. Select one that relates to your leadership responsibility or interest. When all requirements have been met, the diploma will be automatically mailed to your church. No charge will be made for enrollment or diplomas.

Title of diploma	Age group or area
1.	
Title of diploma	Age group or area
2.	

Signature of Pastor, Teacher, or Study Leader | Date

MAIL THIS REQUEST TO →
CHURCH STUDY COURSE AWARDS OFFICE
RESEARCH SERVICES DEPARTMENT
127 NINTH AVENUE NORTH
NASHVILLE, TENNESSEE 37234

FORM-725 (Rev. 7-83)